Praise for

128 QUESTIONS ABOUT ADHD

"A game changer! There is a huge difference between diagnosing ADHD and truly understanding it. Dr. Ned Hallowell and therapist Katherine Snedaker combine the latest research with a passion for helping people see ADHD in a more positive light. The book's simple, engaging format makes it easy to jump in anywhere and start recognizing parts of your own story. The result is a book that will have you nodding in recognition—and probably wiping away a few tears along the way."

—Penn Holderness, *New York Times* bestselling author of *ADHD Is Awesome: A Guide To (Mostly) Thriving With ADHD*

"This book captures something many people with ADHD are searching for: a way to make sense of their story. Compassionate, thought-provoking, and genuinely useful."

—Alex Partridge, host of *ADHD Chatter*, @ADHD_Chatter_Podcast

"Edward Hallowell, MD, a pioneer in making life better for people with ADHD, and his coauthor Katherine Snedaker, LSCW, write for those new and veteran to ADHD. They invite you to look into your rearview mirror to better master what's ahead. Never miss a Hallowell tale."

—Lloyd Sederer, MD, former mental health commissioner for NYC and author of thirteen books and hundreds of articles for print and online publications: www.askdrlloyd.com

"*128 Questions About ADHD* by Katherine Snedaker and Edward Hallowell is a powerful book of self-discovery. I highly recommend it, especially for adults who have no idea whether they might have ADHD, who have been told they 'couldn't possibly' have it, or who have been pathologized or absorbed a stereotyped message about what ADHD is or told it is simply something to be fixed.

"This book is very different from the usual ADHD guides. It is exceptionally well laid out, easy to follow, and truly accessible for a person with ADHD. There are no right or wrong answers—only opportunities to explore yourself and gently consider which of your long-standing traits may actually be related to ADHD.

"The questions go far beyond the traditional lists you typically find in ADHD books. They touch on personality quirks, unique ways of seeing the world, and the full, whole-person experience of living with ADHD. The authors offer a strengths-based, respectful view of adults with ADHD, including real responses from others so you can recognize yourself in their stories.

"This is a wonderfully inviting beginners' book—one that helps you understand and truly see yourself, and then decide, on your own terms, whether you want to take the next step."

—Sari Solden, MS, psychotherapist and author of three books on adult ADHD, including *A Radical Guide for Women with ADHD* (with Michelle Frank, PsyD; revised edition, New Harbinger, expected early 2027)

"This book provides a workbook-like feel that lets the ADHDer see what fits for them. Then it guides them to deepen their understanding with real-world illustrations that help them make sense of their ADHD experience."

—John Ratey, MD, coauthor with Ned Hallowell of the Distraction Series and author of *Spark* and others

128 Questions about ADHD :
A Guided Self-Discovery Journey to Look Back and Move Forward

by Katherine P. Snedaker, LCSW with Edward M. Hallowell, MD

ISBN 979-8-89747-104-1

Edited by Miranda Dillon
Cover design by Catherine Herold

Published by

köehlerbooks™

3705 Shore Drive
Virginia Beach, VA 23455
800-435-4811
www.koehlerbooks.com

128 QUESTIONS ABOUT ADHD

A GUIDED SELF-DISCOVERY JOURNEY TO LOOK BACK AND MOVE FORWARD

Katherine P. Snedaker, LCSW
with Edward M. Hallowell, MD

VIRGINIA BEACH
CAPE CHARLES

When people who have ADHD
are finally able to make sense of their past,
self-love and acceptance are no longer something
they have to work at—
they become possible, natural, and deserved.

These 128 Questions do not *teach* self-love and self-acceptance.
Our hope is that they create the conditions for it.

May this book help you understand where you've been.
May you feel seen and acknowledged.
May that understanding support you in loving yourself as you move forward.

In loving memory of my dad, Ralph E. Sloan, Jr.
–Katherine

TABLE OF CONTENTS

WHY LOOK BACK

SEARCH THE INTERNET, and you will find hundreds of excellent books on ADHD filled with tips, strategies, and tools to help navigate life with ADHD after your diagnosis. While these books can help one move forward, I could not find any that could help someone reevaluate their past. Missing was a book to help a newly diagnosed person—or someone simply ADHD-curious—look back and understand how ADHD may have played a role in their childhood, school experience, and adult years.

You may be asking, "Why look back *now* that I have this diagnosis? Shouldn't my focus be on the future?"

You might feel you don't have the time or energy to look back—that you're already late to the party to understanding your ADHD. For many people, there's a sense of urgency—of being late to the diagnosis, late to get help, late to understanding why they are how they are.

Let me reassure you there is enough time, and one of the most powerful life shifts I have witnessed as a person and as a therapist happens when people pause long enough to reexamine their past through the lens of ADHD. Patterns begin to make sense. Old labels loosen. Self-compassion grows.

Rather than trying to convince you with my own experience, I thought I'd share a few quotes from some brilliant voices who have spoken to the value of looking back in order to move forward.

Not everything that is faced can be changed, but nothing can be changed until it is faced.
—James Baldwin

Until you make the unconscious conscious, it will direct your life and you will call it fate.
—Carl Jung

You can't really know where you are going until you know where you have been.
—Maya Angelou

Life can only be understood backwards; but it must be lived forwards.
—Søren Kierkegaard

Turn your wounds into wisdom.
—Oprah Winfrey

What is not worked through is repeated.
—Alice Miller

Name it to tame it.
—Daniel J. Siegel

When you understand your ADHD, you begin to understand your life.
—Edward M. Hallowell

This book is a tool to help you explore your past—and the highs and lows—that may have been created by your unique brain, as every person's answers will be unique to them. These 128 Questions can help you start making sense of your past—so you can see yourself more clearly, as well as more kindly.

These questions are meant to help you to do the following:

1. **Reflect on how ADHD may have shaped your experiences.** As you move through this book, your story may begin to feel more coherent, your experiences more valid, and your inner voice a little less harsh.

2. **Next, open space for deeper and more honest conversations with friends and your family/partner—the circle of people in your life**. This workbook can help you share your experience with your loved ones and maybe help them see how you are part of a group of people who may struggle with similar issues and have similar strengths.

3. **And in the end, serve as a gateway to find other people with ADHD—a new group of friends and support.** There is something profoundly powerful and healing about being in shared space—virtual or physical—with other people who think this way.

In time, self-blame gives way to self-compassion. And the more challenging aspects of ADHD can be held with care, while the creativity, insight, intensity, and unique strengths we share are not only recognized but genuinely celebrated.

In your own reflection and with others, may you find that humor often lives alongside understanding. Humor is essential to forgiveness. If we can laugh together, we can see our human failings and quiet the criticism that is deep in our core.

May this book help you understand where you've been.

May you feel seen and acknowledged.

And may that understanding support you in loving yourself as you move forward.

—Katherine

CREATING THE 128 QUESTIONS

By Dr. Ned Hallowell

THESE 128 QUESTIONS (updated in 2026 by Katherine) will show you the extensive variety of traits and tendencies that come under the umbrella of the misleading term "ADHD." These questions show the complexity and richness of ADHD that many people never seem to realize.

The first version of these questions came to me in 1997, when I was lamenting the medical definition of ADHD. I felt this definition was all about the negativity and none of the positive aspects of this trait, so I composed a short quiz to provide a feel for ADHD for my book, *Driven to Distraction*.

Later, in 2005, I expanded the quiz to 128 Questions for my next book, *Delivered from Distraction*, which covered more ground, highlighting more negative and positive aspects of the ADHD experience I had learned since my first book.

The 128 Questions are not an official test. Rather, these questions were originally written as an introduction to the general terrain and to showcase the ups and downs when living with ADHD.

Katherine's Conversation with Ned Hallowell

In the fall of 2025, I sat down with Dr. Edward "Ned" Hallowell to discover his original intent with these questions and share the alterations in my update.

As a person with ADHD, the 128 Questions have always stood out to me as a unique tool because the questions encourage the reader to reanalyze their past mistakes, struggles, and successes through the lens of ADHD. Unlike most ADHD books that focus on tips and tricks for changing future behavior, these questions are a way to review one's past.

With Dr. Hallowell's permission, I had been working on updating the 128 Questions for a new generation of adults with ADHD, but in that process, I had some questions of my own.

Creating the 128 Questions

I began by asking Ned what motivated him to create the 128 Questions.

"It came to me the way most things come to me with ADHD," Ned said. "As a flash."

He said he was lying in bed reading *The Boston Globe* when he noticed how limited the medical definition of ADHD was—how deficit-based, how narrow, how little it reflected the real lived experience of positive and negative consequences.

"I wanted something that represented the good and the bad," he said. "A fuller definition. So, I made it a quiz. People with ADHD like quizzes. It took me maybe half an hour."

He tucked it into the manuscript of *Driven to Distraction*, co-authored with Dr. John Ratey, never expecting it to become a therapeutic tool for so many in the ADHD world.

"It was not a highlight of the book. I mean, readers have loved the quiz in the book, but I didn't think of it as anything more than a simple quiz at the time. You were the one who took a quiz and made it into something really amazing with your 128-Question online groups during COVID," replied Ned.

Speaking a Universal Language

I asked Ned if it surprised him that, in our online groups, the 128 Questions had resonated across cultures—from our participants in the US to India, Japan, and Australia. He paused.

"Well, yes and no," he said. "ADHD is second nature to me. But to most people? It's confusing. They hear it and think, *What? Do you mean you can't be on time because you don't have a sense of time?* People think ADHD is a lame excuse. But it is not! It is part of me. It reverberates within me. It's part of who I am."

He emphasized that ADHD is more than the list of symptoms in the medical definition; it is the personality architecture of who someone is.

"That's why I wrote the quiz," he said. "To show how diverse the syndrome is. I don't know any other condition that becomes such a defining part of who a person is."

I agreed, noting that adults with ADHD I know or work with as their therapist don't want their ADHD "removed"—they just want to use its positive aspects better and eliminate the negative aspects, which can ruin one's relationships, health, academics, and career. In the online groups, we had many discussions about the medical term *ADHD* and how it just did not reflect what we believed and experienced.

"That's why you and John Ratey suggested the new name *VAST*," I said.

What Is VAST?

VAST (variable attention stimulus trait) is the term proposed by Hallowell and Ratey, MD, in *ADHD 2.0* to provide a more accurate and strengths-based understanding of ADHD. It highlights the variability of attention, deep interest, creativity, and high responsiveness to meaningful stimulation, framing ADHD as a neurodivergent *trait*, not a deficit or disorder.

"Yes," said Ned, "I hate the term attention-deficit disorder. First, it's wrong, as we don't have a deficit of attention. We have an abundance of attention. Our challenge is to control it. But attention deficit makes it sound like a form of dementia, you know? And it is just an incorrect, wrong, insulting, demeaning term, you know? So, I'd love to get rid of it along with the term 'disorder.' I mean, it's a trait. It is not a disorder any more than being left-handed is a disorder."

I shared our experience in the Clubhouse rooms of many of us wanting a new term for ADHD; however, usually someone would speak up from a country where the term "ADHD" was just starting to take hold in the medical community, and that person would say, "Please don't change the term. We're just starting to have the diagnosis of ADHD recognized in my country, and if the US medical community changes the name, then that will put us back to square one of awareness."

Please note that what ADHD has been called has changed many times over the centuries. See the ADHD terminology chart on the following page.

A Brief History of ADHD

A timeline of how language and understanding evolved

Year	In these years, ADHD was called...	Major Advancements of the Time
Pre-1900		**The Era of the nervous child/moral insanity/"mental instability"**
1775		German physician, Melchior Adam Weikard, describes attention disorders in his medical textbook, Der Philosophische Arzt
1798	**Disease of Attention**	Scottish physician, Sir Alexander Critchton describes "mental restlessness" in his book, *An Inquiry into the Nature and Origin of Mental Derangement*
1845	**Fidgety Philip and Johnny Look-in-the-air**	German psychiatrist, Dr. Heinrich Hoffmann, writes children's book interpreted as an early cases of ADHD, depicts Philipp's motor activity and Johnny's inattentiveness
1900–1940		**The Era of "Bad Behavior" starts as viewing hyperactive children as having lacking moral control or being simply naughty, and by the end of the 1940s, moves towards behavior caused by brain injury**
1902	**Defect of Moral Control**	Pediatrician, Sir George Still, who was called "the father of British pediatrics," published on children with significant inattention, impulsivity, and emotional volatility, noting it was not due to poor environment or low intelligence - scientific starting point of the history of ADHD
1920s	**Organic Drivenness**	A specific pattern of hyperactive and impulsive behavior in children believed to be caused by organic brain damage or dysfunction vs moral control
1930s	**Hyperkinetic Disease of Infancy** **Restless Child Syndrome**	German physicians, Dr. Franz Kramer and Dr. Hans Pollnow, established a concept of the hyperkinetic disease that closely resembles the current concept of ADHD
1937		Discovery of Stimulant Benefits: In the USA, Dr. Charles Bradley treats with Benzedrine (an amphetamine)and his observations of stimulant effects in hyperactive children were revolutionary
1940–1960		**The Era of "Brain Damage" assumed all hyperactive children had "minimal brain damage." This term was eventually dropped because many diagnosed children had no identifiable brain injuries**
1940s	**Brain-injured Child Syndrome** **Minimal Brain Damage (MBD) or Minimal Brain Dysfunction**	
1955		Ritalin: FDA approved methylphenidate (Ritalin) as a treatment for hyperactive behavior
1962		Ritalin: FDA approved for use in children
1960–1980		**Researchers focused solely on hyperactivity, missing many inattentive individuals**
1960s	**Hyperkinetic Impulse Disorder**	Shifting focus from "minimal brain damage" to a functional disorder
1968	**Hyperkinetic Reaction of Childhood**	DSM-II: The American Psychiatric Association (APA) officially recognized the condition
1980–1990		**The shift focused more on inattention, and later recognized that ADHD was not just a childhood condition but often lasted into adulthood.**
1980	**Attention Deficit Disorder (ADD) with/without hyperactivity**	DSM-III: Renamed to ADD, recognizing that hyperactivity was not present in all cases (introduced "with or without hyperactivity")
1987	**Attention Deficit Hyperactivity Disorder (ADHD)**	DSM-III-R: Renamed to ADHD, combining hyperactivity, impulsivity, and inattention into one list of symptoms
1990–1999		**"Subtypes" are added to ADHD**
1994	**ADHD subtypes: Inattentive, Hyperactive-Impulsive, Combined**	DSM-IV: Defined three subtypes: Inattentive, Hyperactive-Impulsive, and Combined
2000–Present		**"Subtypes" changed to "Presentations"**
2013	**ADHD with Presentations**	DSM-5: Reclassified as a neurodevelopmental disorder - updated the symptoms to better apply to adolescents and adults
Current	**ADHD with Presentations**	Research framing ADHD as "Executive Function Disorder" Longitudinal studies have shown ADHD is invariably chronic and not an episodic disorder Twin studies show ADHD is a highly heritable disorder

See References at the end of the book

Getting a Diagnosis

Even after my diagnosis at thirty-six, I continued to mask my ADHD and carry shame. Ned's openness and attitude about his own ADHD helped me begin to see my brain in a positive light—and made me wonder how he had first received his diagnosis.

"I diagnosed myself," he replied. It was 1981, and he was a psychiatry fellow at Harvard, studying child psychology, when he attended a lecture by Dr. Elsie Freeman on ADD.

And he thought, *Whoa—that's me.*

He then described the relief of finally having a name—but there was frustration too.

"The description left out all the good parts," he said. "It missed my essence. And that has been my motivation with my books on ADHD, to always try to fill those parts into the official medical definition."

Ned stated that he never pursued a formal evaluation. "John Ratey agrees I have it. Russ Barkley once said I couldn't have it because I've done too well. I told him, 'Russ—believe me. I have it.'"

Writing a Book on ADHD

Before becoming one of the world's most widely recognized ADHD authors, Ned wrote his first book with a stockbroker on the psychology of money, titled *What Are You Worth?* But when it didn't sell, he was extremely disappointed, but he didn't give up.

"I love writing," he said. "I wrote my first novel in twelfth grade."

While his second book, *Driven to Distraction*, would become an international bestseller, the book's origins were humble. As he was in his fellowship in child psychiatry, Ned started to see pediatric patients who had ADD, and he found that their parents did not seem to know anything about the diagnosis. So in an effort to educate the parents of his patients, he started writing educational handouts—five pages on classroom management, five on non-medication tools, five on couples, families, etc.

He stacked them in piles along the long bookcase in the office he shared with his friend (and later fellow coauthor), Dr. John Ratey. "When I had about fifteen piles, I thought, *Why not turn this into a book?*"

A friend, who was a well-known publisher, was skeptical about the need for the book and the title he chose: *Driven to Distraction*. "Ned, I don't think people are going to know what this book is. *Driven to Distraction*? I don't like it. People are going to think it's a book about cars, or distracted driving, or something like that."

And the friend continued, "Nobody's heard of ADD, so who's going to buy it?"

And yes, very few people had heard of ADD at the time. In the early 1990s, ADHD was often dismissed as laziness, bad parenting, or a nonexistent trend. Even colleagues at the hospital mocked his forthcoming ADD book. A head of the hospital cautioned, "Why write about boys who are pains in the ass?"

Ned was not dismayed. He knew ADHD was more than just being unruly boys, and there's a lot more to ADD than "being a pain in the ass." In the end, Ned was right, and the book, *Driven to Distraction*, along with the sequel, *Delivered from Distraction*, helped shift ADHD from a fringe concept to a globally recognized neurodevelopmental condition.

Ned also spearheaded the recognition of the positive attributes of this kind of brain. "People with ADHD are some of the most creative people in the world. And, in fact, wherever you find dense creativity, entrepreneurialism, and a strong work ethic, you'll find us," said Ned.

When the World "Got It"

I asked when he knew *Driven to Distraction* was catching on.

"Very quickly," he said. "It was like the first line of the book: 'When you understand this condition, you'll see it everywhere.' And that's what happened. People began to see it everywhere."

Ned's publisher originally hoped the book might sell 10,000 copies. Instead, *Driven to Distraction* went on to sell more than one million. When his other ADHD titles are included, total sales exceed two million copies—and his books have now been translated into more than thirty languages around the world.

I asked what he thought we were missing today in ADHD diagnoses, and Ned reflected, "Girls were still grossly underdiagnosed in the past, and we are still missing them today."

Underdiagnosed Girls

For decades, girls with ADHD—especially bright, compliant, and emotionally perceptive girls—were often missed. Their inattentive symptoms were dismissed as daydreaming, anxiety, or "not trying hard enough," while their coping strategies—perfectionism, people-pleasing, overpreparation—hid the real struggle. Many of these girls didn't fall apart until adulthood, when the cost of compensating became unsustainable. This mirrors my own experience: labeled dyslexic at fourteen, not diagnosed with ADHD until years later. Today we know better—and for many women, recognition brings not lateness but long-overdue clarity.

When I told Ned about my experience with the 128 Questions, he said, "I had only thought of it as an alternative definition of ADHD, but it makes sense to me how you used it in your life and in the online groups. We think as adults, *Why was I always late?* It's not because I was inconsiderate. *Why could I never clean up my room?* It's not because I was lazy."

I asked him what he says to people who don't believe in ADHD.

Ned replied, "When people say they don't believe in it, I say to them, 'Look, it's not a religious concept, you know. It's not a matter of believing in it. It's science, and if you don't believe in science, well, that's another problem of its own.'"

The "Group" Experience

During the first two years of COVID, when I ran the online 128 Questions group with my fellow moderators—Grace, Brandy, Godwin, and others—on Clubhouse, we felt a unique emotional power in being surrounded by dozens of other ADHD adults who thought like we did. Our groups often had seventy to eighty participants each night and would typically last ninety minutes. People from every corner of the world joined in, sharing unique answers to each question—but the emotional undercurrent was the same: a deep recognition of shared experience.

Ned had attended several of these online groups, and I asked when else he had experienced being in a group of people with ADHD. He said our Clubhouse groups reminded him of when he attended meetings of CHADD (Children and Adults with Attention-Deficit/Hyperactivity Disorder), a US-based nonprofit dedicated to ADHD advocacy, research translation, and public education.

"There's nothing like being with your group," he said.

A Lasting Legacy

And as a final question, I asked, "How would you like to be remembered?"

"Oh, being a good person," he said. "And I'd love to be remembered as the man who introduced ADHD to the general public. There are plenty of other academics who could claim ADHD books pitched toward an academic audience. I feel, rather than being purely an academic, I would like to be remembered as writing for the people as my audience."

I told him that was already true.

KATHERINE

Finding the 128 Questions

AFTER EIGHT HOURS of neuro-psych testing in 2004, I was diagnosed with ADHD. I was thirty-six years old, married with three children. And in my limited experience, only children were diagnosed with ADHD, not adults. While adults joked about having ADHD, I had never met another person who was diagnosed with ADHD in adulthood.

Since it was before Google, I went to a local bookstore to find a book that could explain what this diagnosis had to do with me. And on a shelf labeled *ADHD*, I found several books, all written by the same expert, Dr. Ned Hallowell. I flipped through the first book from back to front. Too impatient to read the text, I searched for a chart or graphic to explain ADHD to me. And I suddenly came across a quiz in Dr, Hallowell's book and discovered the "128 Questions."

I had wanted to be tested because my six-year-old son had just been diagnosed with ADHD, and in reading his report, I had wondered, *Am I like this too*? My son had been struggling in school, and we paid for testing in hopes of figuring out how to help him. Now, suddenly, I was caught up in the same diagnosis and feeling terrible that "my genetics" appeared to be the cause of his struggles. It was overwhelming to feel like I had to figure this out for myself as fast as I could, so I could get out in front of my ADHD to be able to help my son.

The List That Changed My Life

Once I started reading Dr. Hallowell's list of questions, I don't think I moved until I read all 128. I was struck by how personal they felt. How did Dr. Hallowell know all this about me? The format was simple, just 128 Questions to be answered "yes" or "no." However, the experience was life-changing for me. In the twenty minutes it took me to answer the questions, my awareness of ADHD expanded exponentially, without even reading the book (sorry, Ned!).

These questions uncovered quirky things about myself that I never knew were part of having ADHD, as well as darker aspects of myself that I was completely unaware of and thought were just my secret. But I think the greatest gift of the 128 Questions was highlighting my ADHD strengths (or superpowers), which was not the case in my experience later reading the official medical definition of ADHD, which only outlines the disorder. As I scanned the questions, the aspects of ADHD that really hindered my success (almost like kryptonite to Superman) were mixed in with strengths (superpowers) of which I had not been aware.

This experience helped me fill a void of understanding in a profound way. I am so grateful this was the first definition of ADHD I ever read, and I think it has made all the difference. These questions became my personal definition of ADHD, in turn helping me to raise my son to appreciate the dark and light sides of ADHD.

Meeting Dr. Hallowell

Nine years later, I would meet Dr. Hallowell at a conference in Washington, DC, when we snapped the selfie above. While he does not remember our meeting, for me, it was a rockstar moment to meet the man who gave me my definition of ADHD. I babbled something about how the 128 Questions changed my life and helped me to raise my son, and he was my hero.

A Missed Diagnosis

My own missed diagnosis was not a unique experience in the United States. For decades, girls with ADHD—especially bright, sensitive, and verbally gifted girls—were routinely overlooked, as they did not fit the definition of ADHD at the time. Their symptoms rarely matched the disruptive, hyperactive stereotype built from studies of young boys. Instead of bouncing off walls, many girls turned their restlessness inward and thus were not called out by caregivers and teachers. Their inattentive symptoms were dismissed as *daydreaming*. Emotional dysregulation was labeled *anxiety*. Missed assignments were framed as *carelessness* or *not trying hard enough*. Girls who worked twice as hard to stay afloat were praised for being "good students," even as they exhausted themselves just to keep up.

I was a mix of being hyperactive and criticized often by teachers for not being calm and quiet like the girls. But I was also one who had to secretly work twice as hard, and in some classes, like math and French, no amount of work could raise my grades. And like others, I developed remarkable compensatory strategies: masking, perfectionism, people-pleasing, overpreparation, and quiet compliance. These adaptations helped me survive—and I "thought" helped me keep ADHD hidden. What I did not know until about a decade later is the physical, mental, and emotional cost to try to hide my ADHD, and how really unsuccessful masking was for me.

When I went on ADHD medication, my friends, family, and partner felt I changed in a way that I seemed to be more sincere, made better eye contact, and was more organized and on time (etc.). Research shows that people with ADHD pay a cost to compensate to fit in and hide their ADHD that often shows up later as chronic anxiety, shame, burnout, eating disorders, or depression. And it was hard for me to accept that my masking and (I thought) hiding my ADHD was more of an energy drain and less successful than I had imagined.

My teachers in middle school knew something about me was different and I was struggling to keep up, so my parents switched me to a private school with very small classes. In the smaller, quieter spaces, I felt I could focus better, but despite my efforts to fit in again, I was pulled out for testing when I was fourteen. With this round of testing, I was diagnosed as *"dyslexic"*—an explanation that partially fit, but it didn't tell the whole story. And so it wasn't until I was thirty-six that my ADHD was finally officially diagnosed, and it helped me to look back and reframe my decades of underachievement at certain tasks, self-blame, and unnecessary struggle.

Today, there is more understanding and awareness of how women struggle with ADHD and how hormones, social expectations, and gender norms shape how ADHD appears in girls and women. And in recent years, women with ADHD began to be commonly diagnosed after their children are diagnosed. It is important to realize that a delayed diagnosis doesn't mean delayed impact—it means delayed relief. If you're a woman reading this and thinking, *This sounds uncomfortably familiar*, you're not imagining things and you're not alone.

Men: Identified but Still Misunderstood.

Even though, in some countries with decades of diagnosing males with ADHD, boys and men with ADHD are often *identified,* they are still misunderstood. What in the past was thought of as more of ADHD symptoms of boys—impulsivity, hyperactivity, emotional reactivity—were more likely to draw the criticism of caregivers and teachers rather than compassion.

Rather than being curious, authority figures frequently met these unwanted behaviors with punishment, shame, or labels like he is a "*troublemaker,*" "*lazy,*" or "*defiant.*" When my own children were in elementary school and I volunteered in the school, I was brought to tears more than once when boys with these characteristics suffered the punishment of missed recess and staying inside while their peers got to play outside. I even met with the principal of the school to try to end the practice of "taking away recess," but I was unsuccessful to get this changed, as it was seen as a way to punish children into compliance. Sadly, this punishment takes away much-needed time for ADHD children to be able to exercise, which also provides much-needed mental relief. I can still remember my own elementary school days watching the clock minute by minute until the bell rang for the freedom of recess.

Being Too Much or Not Enough

Studies have shown that many children internalize early messages that they are "too much" or "not enough," leading to chronic self-doubt, anger turned inward or outward, academic disengagement, and higher risk for substance use, legal trouble, and early school dropout. And for boys, emotional vulnerability is often discouraged, leaving fewer outlets for support. Again, this can also be experienced by girls who do not fit the model of the good, quiet students.

And as adults with ADHD, we may struggle silently with follow-through, finances, relationships, and identity—and even for those who were diagnosed as children, ADHD, for years, was framed as a "childhood problem" they were "supposed to outgrow."

In my international discussions with people with ADHD and in my follow-up research, there are many countries where ADHD is not recognized in any form as a medical diagnosis, and thus it is seen as a sign of laziness or poor parenting. Even though ADHD is recognized in other countries, it can vary widely if there is access to testing, follow-up support, and medication. More on this in the next chapter.

128 QUESTIONS GO GLOBAL

SIX YEARS AFTER meeting Ned in Washington, DC, our lives would cross again during the COVID pandemic, in virtual space, on the app Clubhouse. Launched in March of 2020, Clubhouse was a live, audio-only social media platform that became wildly popular during the isolation of the COVID pandemic. On this app, members could host a virtual "room" on any topic, and other members around the world can join the discussion.

I was feeling very isolated during COVID and wanted to host a room. I had always loved running in-person groups in my work as a social worker, and I missed that sense of connection deeply.

My first idea was to open a room on the thirty-six questions from Mandy Len Catron's widely shared article in *The New York Times* called "The 36 Questions That Lead to Love." But when I searched the platform, I saw someone else had already started a room around those questions.

That's when Ned's 128 Questions came to mind. I had long loved sharing them with friends who wondered if they might have ADHD. I had even given them to ADHD-curious clients over the years.

So I quickly pulled out Dr. Hallowell's book and began reading through the questions again.

To my surprise, my own answers had not changed in eighteen years.

And yet, so much in my life *had* changed since the first time I encountered them: I had raised three sons, gone through a divorce, and survived breast cancer.

It struck me then that there was something foundational about these questions. They seemed to reach deeper—touching more on who I was at my core than on what I had experienced across the years.

I became convinced these questions would make an interesting topic to launch a room, so, with a mix of excitement and terror, I opened my first Clubhouse room on the 128 Questions in February 2021. My plan was to pick three or four questions and see if anyone would join, and we would share for fifteen minutes on each question, then move on to the next one.

I was amazed to see the room fill to over seventy members within the first thirty minutes, and with people from all over the world who wanted to share their experiences with ADHD.

It became clear almost immediately that my plan to cover multiple questions per session wasn't realistic. A majority of the people in the room wanted to contribute their thoughts on the very first question, sharing stories, memories, and realizations. That single question filled the entire ninety-minute time slot I had scheduled.

And that set the rhythm of exploring one question a night.

Over the next two years, alongside my deeply committed co-moderators—some of whom you'll meet in this book—we held daily rooms and worked our way through three complete cycles of the 128 Questions. In total, it took nearly 400 days.

During those two years, the 128 Questions were discussed, picked apart, and deeply explored by hundreds of participants from across the globe—Japan, Iran, India, Australia, Saudi Arabia, the United Kingdom, and throughout the European Union. And even when their answers were vastly different, the emotional outcome was strikingly similar: People felt seen, understood, and less alone.

There was something deeply fundamental about what Dr. Hallowell had created! And we found that these questions transcended culture, religion, age, and gender and brought people with ADHD together into a safe, loving community. And we soon learned from our new international friends that ADHD was not recognized in many countries.

More on International Differences in ADHD Diagnosis

ADHD is a globally observed neurodevelopmental condition, but it is not recognized—or treated—the same way in every country. In much of the world, ADHD is formally recognized through established diagnostic systems such as the DSM (used primarily in the United States and Canada) and the ICD (used in many other countries). Nations including the US, Canada, the UK, most of Western and Northern Europe, Australia, Japan, and parts of Latin America have official diagnostic criteria and clinical pathways for ADHD, though access and attitudes vary widely—especially for adults and girls.

In other regions, ADHD may be poorly recognized, inconsistently diagnosed, or functionally invisible within public health systems. This is often due to limited mental health infrastructure, cultural stigma, lack of clinician training, or reliance on outdated psychiatric frameworks. In these settings, ADHD-related traits may be labeled as behavioral problems, character flaws, or moral failings rather than a treatable condition.

Importantly, a lack of recognition does not mean a lack of ADHD. Research suggests ADHD traits occur worldwide at similar rates. What differs is whether a name, an explanation, or support is available. For many adults—especially women—receiving an ADHD diagnosis later in life is not a sign of delay or trendiness. It is often the first time their lifelong experience finally has a framework that makes sense.

Ned Joins Us on Clubhouse

About a month after we started, one of our cohosts from Australia, Grace, decided—right in the middle of a live room—to look up Dr. Hallowell's contact information.

In true ADHD fashion, she reached out to him on the spot, and he answered her email right away!

Then she forwarded me his response, and I quickly emailed him to invite him to join us that night, which he did! He was so excited we were using his questions and was stunned with the size of the community we had built. Over the next two years, it was amazing to have Ned just spontaneously appear in our rooms. And he was very generous with his time, and the room would swell to over 500 people when he would pop in for a topic.

Here is an excerpt from a conversation between Dr. Hallowell and me when he joined one of our Clubhouse rooms in 2023. I said, "What a unique space this is—one where you [Ned] can move in and out freely and share your thoughts not only as one of the world's leading voices on ADHD but also simply as a person among us. I'm deeply grateful for your willingness to share your knowledge and lived experience with a group of people—many of whom you've never met—who are exploring your 128 Questions together."

Dr. Hallowell responded, "You really turn my work into your own, and that's a wonderfully creative act. What you all do in these sessions is truly special. It's a real treat for me to listen and hear the questions come alive through everyone in this room."

While we did not record our rooms on Clubhouse, we did hold a special night in 2022, where we had permission to record comments from the group's members. (The following comments were transcribed from that recording and have been edited only for grammar.)

> "I live outside the United States, and I don't know any adults who are dealing with ADHD openly. The 128 Questions really are very grounding, and I have learned that a lot of us with ADHD need to be grounded. But the 128 Questions are so helpful, so we can be aware of ourselves in a deeper way."

> "I came away with a better understanding of what characteristics are ADHD and perhaps even identified a few new ones with our exchanges along the way. I also came away with confidence about who I am as someone with ADHD and why we are valuable in society, what special gifts we have to offer, realizing the humor in the stories shared between us, and finally, really garnering confidence in ourselves that society has continuously chipped away."

> "The 128 Questions have helped me unpack that paradoxical personality that I lived with. Now, as a person who works with ADHD folks, it has been fantastic to see people come into this room and, through the 128 Questions, uncover and discover their ADHD, allowing them to embark on that interesting journey that brings us all to this community."

> "It helped to identify just how many of the 128 Questions resonated with me; for example, I found 117 of 128 Questions were absolutely true to me and the difficulties I sometimes have with ADHD."

> "Dr. Hallowell and his research have literally saved most of us from what sometimes seemed like a bleak future and outlook, and why, through the 128 Questions, we see things so differently. We have an asset we never realized!"

"Well-meaning families and teachers and even friends gave me wrong advice about how to deal with my ADHD as purely negative. And now I really look at my ADHD as an asset, as well as learned how to best deal with the shortcomings and difficult situations I continually found myself in over the years. So many of them repeatedly, without me understanding why until now."

"Yes, the 128 Questions helped *so* much—in my confidence, my understanding, the positive actions that I *can* take to live an easier, better life without so much second-guessing and berating myself for somehow not measuring up in others' and society's estimation. I still keep in touch with many of the friends I've made and got to know through the 128 Questions. There was a wonderful trust established between us and support that resulted from those questions."

How I Changed

Over those years, I started to change my feelings about my own struggle with ADHD as I shared and connected with the people in our 128 rooms. The critical voice inside my head started to soften as our community grew and I felt a part of this larger group. For example, before being in the rooms, I would mentally beat myself up if I forgot (which I often did) an expensive coffee or a meal on the roof of my car, and in driving away, the coffee cup or salad would fly off the car, littering the road behind me.

After being in 128 rooms, a kinder me would chuckle to myself as the cup flew off the car, and I'd think, *Wow, that was pretty silly and I cannot wait to share this in the room tonight and see who relates*. And later, sharing in the room, other members would laugh and respond with empathy. In connecting with so many wonderful people, my inner voice was becoming less critical and nicer to myself.

Updating the 128 Questions for This Book

During our first round using Dr. Hallowell's 2005 questions, we found that some of the questions had not weathered well with time. Advances in technology, shifts in culture, and a deeper understanding of inclusion made a thoughtful update necessary—one that preserved the spirit of the original questions while reflecting how people live, connect, and understand themselves today.

With Dr. Hallowell's approval and based on the feedback from the rooms, I have updated the questions for a new generation of people with ADHD. I hope this workbook will generate a new way to view one's past, a pathway to a sense of belonging, and a new framework to view ADHD for people across the world.

In my private practice, I use the 128 Questions with my clients who are curious about ADHD or who are seeking a deeper understanding of how it may be shaping their lives. I often introduce the questions as a starting point for our work together, not as a test or diagnosis—but rather an invitation to reflect and an opportunity to notice what resonates.

When I initially assign the questions as homework, clients often approach them with understandable hesitation. Yet in the following session, many arrive having highlighted questions that felt surprisingly familiar and unexpectedly personal—questions that helped them see patterns in their lives, recognize themselves in new ways, and begin talking about their own experience of ADHD.

Through this workbook, I hope you can continue your journey to piece your life experiences together to create a mosaic that makes sense to you. All of you, including the parts of yourself that you may adore and the darker aspects you may wish to hide away: the good, bad, ugly, and beautiful aspects of yourself.

This book would not have been possible without Ned's original 128 Questions and all the moderators and members in the Clubhouse rooms from 2020 to 2022. I am so grateful to have gained a sense of belonging to people like me—and that made all the difference.

HOW TO USE THIS BOOK

1. GO AT YOUR OWN PACE.

This book is a workbook, not a test.
You do not need to answer every question at once—or in order.

Work through a few questions at a time.
Pause when you need to.
Trust what feels manageable for you.

Each of the 128 Questions can be explored in multiple ways. At the top of each page is the question itself, followed by prompts to help you reflect more deeply. You may choose to work through the book in order, or you can return later to any question where you answered "yes" and explore it further.

Once you have answered all 128 Questions, you can count the number of times you marked "yes." Generally, the more questions that resonate with a "yes," the more likely it is that ADHD may be part of your experience. There is no cutoff score—this workbook is descriptive, not diagnostic.

You are also welcome to flip through the book in any order, marking "yes" or "no" as you go, and then return at the end to count your "yes" responses. There is no right or wrong way to use this book—only the way that works best for you.

Next, under each of the 128 Questions, there is a section for deeper exploration with a tool I designed called the "kryptonite to superpower" scale. It looks like the image below.

Kryptonite	**"Neutral"**	**Red Cape**
A trait that hinders/limits	A trait that has no effect	A trait that strengthens/empowers

For each ADHD question, you can decide if a trait hinders (or limits) your life (kryptonite), has no effect (neutral face emoji), or is a strength/superpower (cape).

2. NOTICE WHAT RESONATES.

As you read, some questions may feel

- immediately familiar,
- emotionally charged,
- confusing or surprising, or
- deeply validating.

All of these responses are meaningful. If you have ADHD, you will be surprised by how many questions hit close to home.

If you do not have ADHD (or maybe doubt that ADHD is real), these questions will be a good place to learn more about the many aspects of ADHD.

3. WRITE AS YOU GO.

Write down your thoughts as they arise, even if they feel unfinished.

- You do not need polished answers.
- Brief notes are enough.
- Doodle. Draw a picture.

Capturing your reflections in the moment helps preserve insights that can fade once you move on to the next question.

4. MARK PAGES TO RETURN TO.

Throughout the book, you'll find boxes to check.

Use this to note

- questions that stand out,
- pages you want to revisit, or
- questions you may want to share with someone else.

This makes it easier than trying to remember everything at the end.

5. USE IT TO SUPPORT CONVERSATION.

If you choose, the questions you mark can become

- starting points for therapy sessions,
- ways to explain your experience to a partner, friend, or family member, or
- anchors for group or community discussions.

6. THERE IS NO "RIGHT" OUTCOME.

The goal is not to fix yourself or reach a conclusion.

The goal is to

- recognize patterns,
- make sense of your story, and
- understand yourself with more clarity and kindness.

For many people, confidence and self-compassion grow naturally from there.

7. RETURN ANYTIME.

You can come back to this book

- during different life stages,
- when something feels off, or
- when you want grounding or perspective.

Each time, you may notice something new.

This book works best when you let it meet you where you are.

COMMENTS FROM AROUND THE WORLD

AFTER EACH OF the 128 Questions, you'll find a section where some of the original members of our Clubhouse rooms and others with ADHD share their thoughts.

I hope these responses help you feel the power of these questions—not just in how they invite personal reflection but in how they come alive when people share their experiences openly. Again and again, these conversations have shown how meaningful it can be to hear your own thoughts echoed in someone else's words and to realize you're not alone in what you've felt or how you have struggled. And you can also see how unique each person is in their thoughts.

Reading how others respond can be a gentle reminder that self-compassion often begins in recognition—and that loving yourself with ADHD becomes easier when you see your experiences reflected and understood by others. Some responses have been lightly edited for clarity and length, while preserving the voice and spirit of the original reflections. You'll find brief introductions to the contributors on the following page.

There is no right or wrong way to use this book—only your way. Trust yourself as you move through it.

Brandy lives in the US.
I was thirty-six when my son was tested and diagnosed for ADHD. The psychologist asked which parent also had ADHD, and we pointed at each other! My longtime primary-care doctor agreed. Our household is never boring. I can tell you that! I was thirty-seven or thirty-eight when I went on meds. I was a moderator for the 128 Questions rooms on Clubhouse from 2020 to 2022.

Godwin lives in London.
I was diagnosed at the age of thirty-three, in 2006. I was a moderator for the 128 Questions rooms on Clubhouse from 2020 to 2022.

Claudia Belinda was born in Peru, now living in the US.
I was diagnosed at the age of fifty. I was a member of the 128 Questions room on Clubhouse from 2020 to 2022.

Toshi lives in Japan.
I was diagnosed with ADHD at forty-eight at the same time my son was diagnosed with ADHD. I run two after-school day cares for neurodiverse children—mainly kids with ADHD and ASD—and we currently have about 100 students. I was a member of the 128 Questions rooms on Clubhouse.

Muniqui is a US citizen living in Japan for the last twenty-five years.
I was diagnosed at the age of twenty-two. I was a member of the 128 Questions rooms on Clubhouse from 2020 to 2022.

Austin lives in San Francisco's Castro, a nationally recognized LGBTQ+ cultural heritage neighborhood.

I was diagnosed at age six. I am the director of Block Island Pride, where I lead community-centered programming and celebration that uplifts queer visibility, connection, and joy. I was not a member of Clubhouse.

Sara lives in the US.

I was a member of the 128 Questions clubhouse room and started the ADHD & Relationships room on Clubhouse. I own a coaching business.

Nathan lives in Minneapolis, MN, with his family.

I was a member of the 128 Questions clubhouse room, which was instrumental in leading me to get diagnosed with ADHD at forty-one years old. I am a sculptor and visual artist.

128 QUESTIONS

Kryptonite
A trait that hinders/limits

“Neutral”
A trait that has no effect

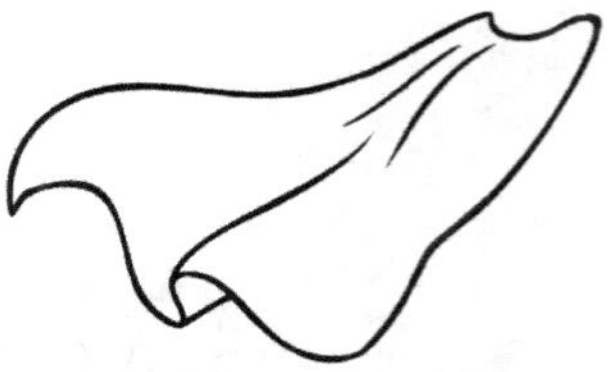

Red Cape
A trait that strengthens/empowers

Do you get annoyed when someone gives you directions with more than three steps?

☐ YES
☐ NO

If yes, does getting annoyed . . .			
• Affect your ability to remember the directions?	☐	☐	☐
• Play a role in your relationship(s) at home?	☐	☐	☐
• Show up in your work/school life?	☐	☐	☐
• Impact your ability to successfully complete a task?	☐	☐	☐

If you need to ask for instructions, which would you prefer?

☐ Verbal
☐ Written
☐ A drawing/photo

Share this page with . . .

☐ Family/Partner
☐ Friend
☐ Doctor
☐ Therapist/Coach/Support Group

Do you get annoyed when someone gives you directions with more than three steps?

Brandy: I don't think I get annoyed, but if it's more than three steps, it's really hard for me to follow. I lose my train of thought after the third one. Anything past three steps, I would probably have to take notes.

Godwin: I don't get annoyed. I can usually intuitively find my way to where I want to go because I don't really like asking people for advice.

Belinda: No, not really, because I prefer more details because I tend to get lost quite easily and need help.

Austin: I try my best to follow the directions and ask follow-up questions if I get lost. I do get frustrated with myself when I go to do the task and forget the steps or realize that I have done my own process. It has made me a better self-starter and independent person as I try to rely on my problem-solving skills rather than give up and ask for help.

Toshi: No, I don't get annoyed. I just start to lose focus after the third step, but I still appreciate the explanation.

Muniqui: Yes, if I ask someone, "How do I boil water?" and the answer they give could fit in a twelve-volume edition of the Encyclopedia Britannica.

Sara: No, but I'm almost certainly going to repeat them back to make sure I got it.

Nathan: I used to, but now I politely wait for them to finish before letting them know that I will need them to repeat everything after I've completed step one. When successful, this approach results in them doing it themselves or finding someone else to do it.

Q 2

Do you feel that you are underachieving in your life, even though you may have achieved a great deal so far?

☐ YES
☐ NO

If yes, how does your feeling of "underachieving in life" . . .

• Affect how you feel about yourself?	☐	☐	☐
• Play a role in your relationship(s)?	☐	☐	☐
• Show up in your work/school life?	☐	☐	☐
• Impact your ability to make future plans?	☐	☐	☐

What are some areas in your life where you have a feeling of not having achieved what you wanted?

Where do you feel you have achieved a great deal?

Share this page with . . .

☐ Family/Partner
☐ Friend
☐ Doctor
☐ Therapist/Coach/Support Group

Do you feel that you are underachieving in your life, even though you may have achieved a great deal so far?

Brandy: Absolutely.

Godwin: Yeah, if I look at the present time, I'm underachieving because I'm avoiding a lot of things. But if I look back honestly, yes. I've done some pretty cool things, but I just haven't maintained them over time. *LOL*.

Belinda: Yes, I used to be a bit tough on myself because I'm an immigrant and my parents had high expectations. The last two years have been personally challenging (raising a child with special needs alone, grieving the traumatic losses of two loved ones, and dealing with divorce). It wasn't easy, but I made it to the other side. I feel empowered and look forward to a better future.

Austin: Absolutely. I did really well in school and got an amazing degree, but I have really failed to secure stable, long-term work that I enjoy.

Toshi: Yes. And now I have a place where I belong. After a long journey, I've finally found a place where I can build something of my own and keep giving my best until the very end. For people with ADHD, independence is essential. Even when the work is hard and the risks are high, freedom and autonomy are what allow us to truly come alive. The scale of the business doesn't matter—ADHD minds cannot survive without independence.

Muniqui: Absolutely! Yes. I have not written books I wanted to write. I don't have any savings to fall back on, and I feel like I have a Maserati engine of a brain and I'm only able to produce results at bicycle speeds.

Sara: Sadly, only in the last couple of years have I come to this conclusion. It's slightly depressing, but at the same time, I've done so many wonderful and creative things that I'm proud of, and I try to live without regret.

Nathan: Yes—in almost every area of my life.

Q 3

Are you more generous than most people?

☐ YES
☐ NO

If yes, how does being generous . . .

• Affect how you feel about yourself?	☐	☐	☐
• Play a role in your relationship(s)?	☐	☐	☐
• Show up in your work/school life?	☐	☐	☐
• Impact your ability to make future plans?	☐	☐	☐

When have you really enjoyed being generous?

Are there examples in your life when you have been too generous?

Do some people take advantage of your generosity?

Share this page with . . .

☐ Family/Partner
☐ Friend
☐ Doctor
☐ Therapist/Coach/Support Group

Are you more generous than most people?

Brandy: Yes, I am more generous than most people. I often jump in to help others out and really enjoy doing this, often even if it means neglecting doing something I should be doing for myself.

Godwin: Yeah, I think I am. I'm always willing to help people, even if sometimes I really don't want to.

Belinda: Yes, to a fault. If it's raining out and there's an unhoused person on the sidewalk, I'll hand them my umbrella and some cash.

Austin: I go through phases of selfishness and selflessness. They tend to be on the extremes, and I have had to work to find a better balance.

Toshi: I think so. Because I have about twenty employees and about a hundred students, and I believe I have a responsibility to be honest and generous with them.

Muniqui: I'm balanced in this area.

Sara: *Yes*, and wow, I actually forgot this was part of it. This is going to be extremely eye-opening, isn't it?

Nathan: Yes.

Do you find it harder than most people to stay on track when something doesn't fully hold your attention?

☐ YES
☐ NO

If yes, what degree does having trouble staying on track . . .

• Affect how you feel about yourself?	☐	☐	☐
• Play a role in your relationship(s)?	☐	☐	☐
• Show up in your work/school life?	☐	☐	☐
• Impact your ability to make future plans?	☐	☐	☐

What are the most boring tasks you avoid?

Have you discovered anything that helps you stay on track with a task when you are completely bored?

Share this page with . . .

☐ Family/Partner
☐ Friend
☐ Doctor
☐ Therapist/Coach/Support Group

Do you find it harder than most people to stay on track when something doesn't fully hold your attention?

Brandy: Yes, every day. If it's a boring meeting, I have to start doodling in order to pay attention because I lose focus and drift off. I find if I doodle or write down the things that the person is saying, I can at least stay in the moment; otherwise, I'm out.

Godwin: Let's say affirmative.

Belinda: Yes, I find it extremely difficult to focus on one thing at a time. It feels like life is a chess game, and I need to be a few moves ahead.

Austin: I definitely have problems staying on track, but I have learned that I can self-medicate with caffeine, so I need to focus on doing mentally taxing tasks at certain parts of the day, like in the morning. I tend to work best from 9 a.m. to 3 p.m., and at that time, I try to eliminate all distractions, focus on my work, and drink lots of coffee.

Toshi: Yes, I do. I have trouble staying on track, especially when I'm not interested. ADHD medication may help with staying on track, but when something interests me, I have no trouble at all with my attention.

Muniqui: Yes.

Sara: I think so, yes. I see that come up the most at work. (*Shhhh.*)

Nathan: Absolutely. The moment something ceases to interest me, I look for the nearest exit. If removing myself isn't an option, I occupy myself with other things while doing my best impression of a person paying attention.

Do you feel some regrets about the way you are but also feel unable to find any way to change?

☐ YES
☐ NO

If yes, what degree does "being unable to change" . . .

• Affect how you feel about yourself?	☐	☐	☐
• Play a role in your relationship(s)?	☐	☐	☐
• Show up in your work/school?	☐	☐	☐
• Impact your ability to make future plans?	☐	☐	☐

What are some examples of regrets you have?

What would you like to change about your life if there were no barriers to change?

Share this page with . . .

☐ Family/Partner
☐ Friend
☐ Doctor
☐ Therapist/Coach/Support Group

Do you feel some regrets about the way you are but also feel unable to find any way to change?

Brandy: Yes. yes. And yes. And that is such a strange kind of place to be.

Godwin: I do have some regrets about the way I am, but it's not that I'm unable to find ways to change, because I know the ways to change logically. I just don't know how to put them into action. As Russell Barclay said, "I know what to do. I don't do what I know."

Belinda: No, I don't feel any regrets. That's how I'm wired. I was born with what I call a "beautiful brain." I wouldn't change it even if I could. I see it in my dad, in one of my brothers, and in my son. It's truly a gift.

Austin: I know that I have these patterns. I'm really grateful that when I was a child, my mom invested in getting me an ADHD diagnosis and tried out medications and helped me identify these issues in my life. And I have been able to build coping mechanisms and practices for the rest of my life.

Toshi: Yes. I do. I understand it, but I respond instinctively before I even notice it. The outcomes of those instinctive reactions can be either good or bad—it feels like a "gotcha."

Muniqui: Totally, yes.

Sara: Some regrets, yes, but I like my direct, interrupting, dare I say, sassy approach? I wouldn't have it any other way.

Nathan: No. I have harnessed my ADHD into a superpower and would not change it even if I could.

Would you have made a good inventor?

☐ YES
☐ NO

If yes, how does being able to invent/create. . .			
• Affect how you feel about yourself?	☐	☐	☐
• Play a role in your relationship(s)?	☐	☐	☐
• Show up in your work/school life?	☐	☐	☐
• Impact your ability to make future plans?	☐	☐	☐

What are some examples when you have invented something or figured out something new?

How do you feel when you *must* do things a particular, regimented way instead of being creative or inventive?

Share this page with . . .

☐ Family/Partner
☐ Friend
☐ Doctor
☐ Therapist/Coach/Support Group

Would you have made a good inventor?

Brandy: I'm not sure. I'd like to create things, but I don't like to be the first one, so I don't know about being a good inventor. My philosophy is that I like to see it in action. I'm not going to be the first person to buy that new car, that new model, because usually, there are bugs that need to be worked out. I'm going to sit back and watch what happens.

Godwin: No, I don't think so. Because of all the reiterations that you have to do, I'd probably give up after the first go, but I'm a good ideas man.

Belinda: Yes, but I would've started from the mindset of "What can I invent to improve X, Y, or Z?"

Austin: I think going back to my skills as a self-starter and having to figure puzzle things out for myself, I have become a scrappy and inventive person who can create a lot with little and, when put into tricky situations, can tend to find my way out and find the light.

Toshi: Yes, no matter the situation, I usually end up coming up with very good ideas, though sometimes it goes the other way. What I truly dislike is being forced to follow rigid systems or standard methods that leave no room for creativity.

Muniqui: No.

Sara: No. I feel like inventors are handy, and I'm not handy.

Nathan: I am a great inventor.

Do you perceive patterns where other people don't see them?

☐ YES
☐ NO

If yes, how does your perception of patterns . . .			
• Affect how you feel about yourself?	☐	☐	☐
• Play a role in your relationship(s)?	☐	☐	☐
• Show up in your work/school?	☐	☐	☐
• Impact your ability to make future plans?	☐	☐	☐

What are some examples of when you've seen patterns with people, numbers, or ideas?

How do you wish you could use this skill?

Share this page with . . .

☐ Family/Partner
☐ Friend
☐ Doctor
☐ Therapist/Coach/Support Group

Do you perceive patterns where other people don't see them?

Brandy: I try to find patterns. And I feel like there are patterns in everything.

Godwin: I don't know about patterns but can work out things that others can't or don't realize. Oh, and I see shapes of faces in objects.

Belinda: Yes, in numbers, symbols, even in other people's behaviors. Seeing patterns in behaviors was very helpful when I worked as a victim advocate for children of abuse.

Austin: I'd say yes for random subjects and topics, but then for more general things that other people pick up on more quickly, I have a slower and harder time, especially if I'm not interested in the subject.

Toshi: Yes, I do. And sometimes I notice patterns in the world around me—across everything happening—not just in myself. I can see these patterns instantly at times.

Muniqui: Yes, yes, and yes. All the time. Sometimes the pattern's extremely obvious and I don't see why others don't see them.

Sara: I don't think I do, unless we're talking about human connection. I think I'm extra perceptive about reading people.

Nathan: Yes. I believe that elite pattern recognition is one of the most positive byproducts of my ADHD.

Do you tend to solve problems intuitively rather than logically and methodically?

☐ YES
☐ NO

If yes, how does your way of solving problems . . .

• Affect how you feel about yourself?	☐	☐	☐
• Play a role in your relationship(s)?	☐	☐	☐
• Show up in your work/school?	☐	☐	☐
• Impact your ability to make future plans?	☐	☐	☐

What are some examples in your life?

Have there been times when you wished you were more logical?

Share this page with . . .

☐ Family/Partner
☐ Friend
☐ Doctor
☐ Therapist/Coach/Support Group

Do you tend to solve problems intuitively rather than logically and methodically?

Brandy: I go with my gut, and I think people with ADHD are usually quick thinkers, and we have to learn to adapt quickly because we might zone out or miss something, and we've learned to kind of read the room and figure things out.

Godwin: Yes, my answer is usually "Don't ask me how I did it."

Belinda: Yes and no. I go with my intuition first, then look at the problem with logic and method. Whenever I've gone against my intuition, I've been burned or made a big mistake.

Austin: I think, as a child and in my earlier life, I was more intuitive with the way that I engaged with tasks because I had a hard time following directions and would create my own pathways to solving problems. As an adult, I've built better practices and been more introspective, and I can now do things logically and methodically, but that is more of an active practice than something that I would do naturally.

Toshi: Yes. That's why I can't solve puzzle rings at all. I guess I need to think more carefully and more logically.

Muniqui: I use both intuitive and logical thinking.

Sara: Absolutely. Just thinking about reading an instruction manual makes me want to lie down.

Nathan: Not necessarily. I am both intuitive and methodical. When that doesn't work, I just avoid the problem altogether.

Q 9

Do you find you hold on to perceived or actual criticisms or rejection more deeply and longer than you imagine other people do?

☐ YES
☐ NO

If yes, how does not being seen as logical by others . . .			
• Affect how you feel about yourself?	☐	☐	☐
• Play a role in your relationship(s)?	☐	☐	☐
• Show up in your work/school?	☐	☐	☐
• Impact your ability to make future plans?	☐	☐	☐

How long do you tend to hold on to these feelings after perceived or actual criticisms or rejection? And what helps shorten this time frame?

Are you able to share with people you trust that you are sensitive to criticism and rejection?

Share this page with . . .

☐ Family/Partner
☐ Friend
☐ Doctor
☐ Therapist/Coach/Support Group

Do you find you hold on to perceived or actual criticisms or rejection more deeply and longer than you imagine other people do?

Brandy: Criticism, sort of, if I feel it's valid. Rejection lasts forever! I don't openly dwell on it, but it's always in the back of my mind.

Godwin: Yes, but I have learned it's because I don't check the facts (I probably wouldn't believe it if I did), so I'm left with uncertainty and resentment. They say misery loves company. I can definitely be good company!

Belinda: Yes, I'll take things personally if I feel criticized or rejected. I may speak with the other person for clarity. If it's an actual criticism or rejection, I defer to the saying, "An elephant never forgets."

Austin: It does take me a minute to overcome harsh criticism and rejection. I meditate on it and try to figure out what went wrong or what I did or what they did or what could've been done better, but I've been doing a lot of mindfulness and to try to unload some of these bad habits and to be more carefree and let things just be and try not to let anybody's negativity tarnish my shine.

Toshi: Yes, I do. Even if I seem to move on outwardly, I may continue to replay it internally. In particular, feelings of rejection tend to stay with and be hard to forget, lingering for a long time afterward.

Muniqui: Yes. Because it really feels like I'm being cut deep and I don't deserve it, and the other people feel like they're being insensitive to my feelings, and they are not understanding where I'm coming from, but I'm expected to understand them.

Sara: I don't think so. I do hold onto criticism in this way, but I think so many people do.

Nathan: I do. It took me a while to acknowledge this truth about myself because I didn't want it to be true. Getting better acquainted with myself has helped me become much less dependent on external validation or approval. But it's an ongoing process. In this moment, I'm aware of my desire for my answers to these questions to be helpful (while attempting to sound smart and funny).

Do you value certain qualities you have, regretting that you can't always present them in such a way that other people appreciate them?

☐ YES
☐ NO

If yes, how does this lack of appreciation of you . . .			
• Affect how you feel about yourself?	☐	☐	☐
• Play a role in your relationship(s)?	☐	☐	☐
• Show up in your work/school?	☐	☐	☐
• Impact your ability to make future plans?	☐	☐	☐

What qualities about yourself do you wish people could see?

Why do you think people miss these qualities in you?

Share this page with . . .

☐ Family/Partner
☐ Friend
☐ Doctor
☐ Therapist/Coach/Support Group

Do you value certain qualities you have, regretting that you can't always present them in such a way that other people appreciate them?

Brandy: Yes. I am really a creative and thoughtful person. However, because it's so hard to focus and meet deadlines, even self-imposed, I am often left with a product or experience that is lacking the finishing touches or looks rushed, instead of the "perfect" picture or plan I had in my head.

Godwin: Yeah, I do. I do have some qualities, but then qualities with inconsistency aren't really a good match, so people don't tend to see my qualities.

Belinda: Yes, it can be a satisfying secret to be neurodivergent before anyone notices that I may be different from the norm. However, it's frustrating when others don't understand my way of thinking. It bothers me the most when it's a loved one or close friend who doesn't get me.

Austin: I think many of my core traits and most interesting aspects are things that I do in private. I spend a lot of time alone doing personal work, reading, doing art, and these are harder things to weave into conversation unless I have a hyperfixation on something, and I think that can also be difficult for people to engage with socially, so I tend to keep those things to myself and to people who know me best, and the people who get to see those things generally appreciate my perspectives and my art.

Toshi: Yes. Especially when I feel someone is misunderstanding me.

Muniqui: This is so me. Yes.

Sara: Not necessarily.

Nathan: No.

Q 11

Are you more tenacious and persistent than the average person?

☐ YES
☐ NO

If yes, how does being so tenacious and persistent . . .

• Affect how you feel about yourself?	☐	☐	☐
• Play a role in your relationship(s)?	☐	☐	☐
• Show up in your work/school?	☐	☐	☐
• Impact your ability to make future plans?	☐	☐	☐

What are some examples of when this quality was not appreciated?

What are some examples of when this was very helpful?

Share this page with . . .

☐ Family/Partner
☐ Friend
☐ Doctor
☐ Therapist/Coach/Support Group

Are you more tenacious and persistent than the average person?

Brandy: Yes. Very persistent. Very tenacious. And I'm persistent when I want something, and I've been that way since I was little.

Godwin: Umm, it depends on what is going on. I can be persistent in arguments, to a fault.

Belinda: Yes, I don't believe in the word "impossible." I've always been a rebel, so if someone tells me I can't do something, I internally say, "Watch me." Even a small improvement to a problem is better than nothing.

Austin: I think that I have to be this way as a coping mechanism. I need to be tenacious and persistent in order to get what seems to come easier for other (non-ADHD) people—like getting a job.

Toshi: Yes. But once I decide something is over, I have no regrets, no matter how much passion I put into it.

Muniqui: No.

Sara: Yes. I'm the one who will stay late to tweak and tweak and edit and edit until it's just right.

Nathan: Yes, for things I care about. Quite the opposite for things I don't.

Q 12

Are you more sentimental than the average person?

☐ YES
☐ NO

If yes, how does being very sentimental . . .			
• Affect how you feel about yourself?	☐	☐	☐
• Play a role in your relationship(s)?	☐	☐	☐
• Show up in your work/school?	☐	☐	☐
• Impact your ability to make future plans?	☐	☐	☐

What are some examples of when this quality was not appreciated?

What are some examples of when this was very helpful?

Share this page with . . .

☐ Family/Partner
☐ Friend
☐ Doctor
☐ Therapist/Coach/Support Group

Are you more sentimental than the average person?

Brandy: Yes, I've always been one to keep photos and memorabilia of my family/partner and friend groups. I am also sentimental about music, as Father was a musician and I listened to a lot of music since I was little. Now when I hear an old song, I can still remember what was going on or how I felt when I first listened to that song.

Godwin: This is a good question. I'm sentimental in the present. But I'm not sentimental in general, because I don't do that whole nostalgia thing. Because my memory was probably elsewhere at the time, and because I was too busy being anxious to even enjoy the moment.

Belinda: Yes, I've always felt things more deeply than others. Music or movies feel like I'm inside them, feeling the notes played or what a character is going through in a scene. It's a higher level of empathy. There's a strong connection to nature and animals too.

Austin: I'm pretty sentimental and I keep lots of photos and write journals. I try to keep up with friendships, and those sorts of things are important to me. I do experience nostalgia for past phases of my life.

Toshi: Yes. I've grown more sentimental as I get older.

Muniqui: Not really. No.

Sara: Yes. I can't watch certain shows that hurt my heart.

Nathan: I'd say I'm very nostalgic. I place a high value and hold on to little things that remind me of important moments. Throwing things away (that hold meaning to me) is difficult, even when they are no longer useful.

Q 13

Do you have an unusually acute sense of smell and/or sensitivity to touch?

☐ YES
☐ NO

If yes, how does this trait . . .

• Affect how you feel about yourself?	☐	☐	☐
• Play a role in your relationship(s)?	☐	☐	☐
• Show up in your work/school life?	☐	☐	☐
• Impact your ability to be intimate with others?	☐	☐	☐

What is an example of when this trait created a barrier for you to connect to another person?

Are there times when this trait is an asset to you?

Share this page with . . .

☐ Family/Partner
☐ Friend
☐ Doctor
☐ Therapist/Coach/Support Group

Do you have an unusually acute sense of smell and/or sensitivity to touch?

Brandy: I don't know if it's unusually acute, but I can pick up on smells. I'm always trying to figure out where I am and what's going on. So that includes smelling what's in the room with me.

Godwin: Yes, I have an acute sense of smell, but not in the sense that I can smell the roses. However, touch is also a touchy subject, pardon the pun.

Belinda: Yes, my nose is like a bloodhound's. I thought it was heightened because my vision is so bad. As a kid, I couldn't go down the detergent aisle in a grocery store, because I'd feel like I would suffocate. As far as touch, turtlenecks felt like they'd choke me. I still can't lie on grass, or I feel itchy. From time to time, I experience flare-ups of chronic pelvic pain and prefer to retreat into my own imaginary bubble. The slightest brush on any part of my skin will cause pain all over my body.

Austin: I do not have an acute sense of smell, as I mostly lost my sense of smell during COVID. I used to have a very intense aversion to perfumes and artificial smells, but I am more sensitive to touch and fabric, especially in clothing.

Toshi: No, I don't have particularly acute senses.

Muniqui: No.

Sara: No, not particularly, but my love language is very clearly touch/snuggle/hug.

Nathan: Yes! I am very sensitive to certain materials and sensations. I once caught a hangnail in a ball of yarn as a child and still have a difficult time touching it to this day.

Q 14

When you are sitting, do you frequently drum your fingers on the table or bounce one of your legs up and down?

☐ YES
☐ NO

If yes, how does having to be in motion . . .			
• Affect how you feel about yourself?	☐	☐	☐
• Play a role in your relationship(s)?	☐	☐	☐
• Show up in your work/school?	☐	☐	☐
• Impact your ability to travel?	☐	☐	☐

How does this affect your relationship with other people in quiet and still spaces?

What are some examples of how you can find ways to move when you cannot leave your seat?

Share this page with . . .

☐ Family/Partner
☐ Friend
☐ Doctor
☐ Therapist/Coach/Support Group

When you are sitting, do you frequently drum your fingers on the table or bounce one of your legs up and down?

Brandy: Yes. Definitely.

Godwin: I used to, but now I have discovered the miracle of a swivel chair.

Belinda: Yes, one of my legs *must* bounce while I'm sitting down.

Austin: I'm a nail biter, and I chew on the inside of my cheek.

Toshi: Yes, very often. And my two brothers also bounce their legs. When all three of us are together, we all bounce at the same time—and my mother goes crazy and screams, "Stop it!"

Muniqui: Yes!

Sara: No, I see this around me a lot with people with ADHD, but it's not my MO.

Nathan: No.

Q 15

Do you love crossword puzzles, brainteasers, and self-assessment quizzes?

☐ YES
☐ NO

If yes, how does your love of puzzles and quizzes . . .			
• Affect how you feel about yourself?	☐	☐	☐
• Play a role in your relationship(s)?	☐	☐	☐
• Show up in your work/school life?	☐	☐	☐
• Impact your ability to get boring tasks done?	☐	☐	☐

What are some examples of analog puzzles and quizzes you like?

What are some examples of digital puzzles and quizzes you like?

Share this page with . . .

☐ Family/Partner
☐ Friend
☐ Doctor
☐ Therapist/Coach/Support Group

Do you love crossword puzzles, brainteasers, and self-assessment quizzes?

Brandy: I love puzzles, etc., especially brainteasers, word finds, and hidden objects. Those are my favorite.

Godwin: I don't think I like crosswords, but I seem to be good at them for some reason. I'm really good at trivia, such as for pub quizzes; I know a lot about nothing, and I'm also good at self-assessment. Still trying to find out what's wrong with me.

Belinda: Yes, they're fun and good for the brain.

Austin: I was a big sudoku fan.

Toshi: I don't like crossword puzzles or brainteasers, but I am interested in self-assessment quizzes, including fortune-telling.

Muniqui: No.

Sara: Yes, I love them, especially word puzzles.

Nathan: Hard pass on the first two. My brain feels teased enough by basic tasks already. But I do enjoy a good self-assessment quiz.

Q 16

Do you love bicycles (even if you don't ride them anymore)?

☐ YES
☐ NO

If yes, how does this . . .

• Affect how you feel about yourself?	☐	☐	☐
• Play a role in your relationship(s)?	☐	☐	☐
• Show up in your work/school life?	☐	☐	☐
• Impact your ability to travel?	☐	☐	☐

Why do you like bikes?

Do you love the spinning of the wheels, the motion, or both?

Share this page with . . .

☐ Family/Partner
☐ Friend
☐ Doctor
☐ Therapist/Coach/Support Group

Do you love bicycles (even if you don't ride them anymore)?

Brandy: I would love to have a bike again. Actually, when I was in Saudi, I had one of those tricycles with the basket on the back and loved riding it. But I don't necessarily want to be on a ten-speed now because I don't want to fall.

Godwin: I do. And I just pumped up my bicycle tires a couple of days ago with the promise of riding it. We'll leave that there.

Belinda: Yes, I love bicycles. I need to upgrade my bicycle and start riding it again.

Austin: I love to ride my e-bike around San Francisco. It's my primary mode of transport. It was my primary mode of transport when I lived in Japan as well. I curated a social group around bike riding when I lived there as well.

Toshi: Yes. I feel a sense of freedom when I ride. I especially love going downhill.

Muniqui: No. Can't ride.

Sara: I do ride, and I do love bicycles.

Nathan: Absolutely. It reminds me of the first taste of true freedom as a kid. The open road, wind blowing through my hair, pure possibility ahead.

Q 17

Do you feel that your accomplishments in life were by accident, by smoke and mirrors, almost as if someone else achieved them, not you?

☐ YES
☐ NO

If yes, how does this feeling of "achievement by accident" . . .

• Affect how you feel about yourself?	☐	☐	☐
• Play a role in your relationship(s)?	☐	☐	☐
• Show up in your work/school?	☐	☐	☐
• Impact your ability to make future decisions?	☐	☐	☐

Would you call this "being lucky," or does it feel more like imposter syndrome?

Is this really true?

Share this page with . . .

☐ Family/Partner
☐ Friend
☐ Doctor
☐ Therapist/Coach/Support Group

Do you feel that your accomplishments in life were by accident, by smoke and mirrors, almost as if someone else achieved them, not you?

Brandy: Yes. Yes.

Godwin: Not really. I think some of it was probably done intuitively. And when I was less anxious about things, I couldn't tell you how I did them, but I know that I've done them.

Belinda: No, I feel the positives I've accomplished were purposeful. However, they weren't to 100 percent of my full capacity.

Austin: There is a driving force in me that I have followed my whole life. Not always toward money, but definitely by passions.

Toshi: Yes. They all felt like accidents and luck. I have always been lucky.

Muniqui: No.

Sara: No, I think I worked hard for them and I'm proud of them. I'm grateful I feel this way.

Nathan: Yes. I tend to view successes as blessings that happened to me and failures as things I caused. Hold on . . . is this therapy? I have more work to do.

Q 18

Do you put up a good front but inwardly wish you could find a better way in life?

☐ YES
☐ NO

If yes, how does this secret wish . . .			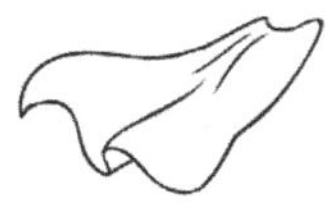
• Affect how you feel about yourself?	☐	☐	☐
• Play a role in your relationship(s)?	☐	☐	☐
• Show up in your work/school?	☐	☐	☐
• Impact your ability to make future plans?	☐	☐	☐

What are some examples of how you put up a good front?

What is it that you wish for?

Share this page with . . .

☐ Family/Partner
☐ Friend
☐ Doctor
☐ Therapist/Coach/Support Group

Do you put up a good front but inwardly wish you could find a better way in life?

Brandy: Yes, hundred percent.

Godwin: Obviously, I need to add some sarcasm here, so, of course not.

Belinda: I put up a good front because, as Shakespeare said, "All the world's a stage." Inwardly, the only thing I wish is that my health was better. Ten years ago, I had a life-altering car accident.

Austin: I don't put up a front. But sometimes I close down socially when I'm overstimulated. Career is a major source of insecurity in my life.

Toshi: Yes. I'm always looking for a better way in life.

Muniqui: Yes.

Sara: Oh, yes. Everyone knows I'm a badass boss lady, but there are certain things I'm quite vulnerable about, and the people closest to me know it.

Nathan: I sometimes believe the lie that my positive qualities are a contrived performance. I am at peace when I accept that I have found a better way to live authentically.

Q 19

Do you go off on tangents easily?

☐ YES
☐ NO

If yes, how does going off on tangents . . .

• Affect how you feel about yourself?	☐	☐	☐
• Play a role in your relationship(s)?	☐	☐	☐
• Show up in your work/school?	☐	☐	☐
• Impact your ability to make future plans?	☐	☐	☐

When do you go off on tangents?

What are some examples of when this is helpful?

Share this page with . . .

☐ Family/Partner
☐ Friend
☐ Doctor
☐ Therapist/Coach/Support Group

Do you go off on tangents easily?

Brandy: Absolutely. I try to make one or two notes if I have to speak to keep me on track. I always doodle or take notes when I'm in meetings or on calls to help keep my focus.

Godwin: Well, I wouldn't call them tangents because there is a connection. I find that other people go off on tangents.

Belinda: Yes, all the time! Last night, my son asked me why I always go off on tangents.

Austin: Yes. I used to do it a lot more but try to redirect conversations back to other people equally when in conversation. I feel like there's a scale that people are on between asking questions and speaking, and sometimes I find myself on the extremes and actively have to try to balance the scale by asking questions or sharing more, and sometimes it's really hard for me to do that.

Toshi: Yes. When something interests me, it triggers my instinct, and my ideas start to flow.

Muniqui: Yes, I do.

Sara: Are you kidding me? Yes. So much, yes.

Nathan: This one time, I was backpacking with my brother, and a bear with her cub came to our campsite to check out what we were eating for dinner. It was crazy. We had to yell and throw rocks for like five minutes before they finally went away. Anyway, what was the question?

On the other hand, do you get really annoyed when other people go off on tangents, wishing they'd hurry up and get to the point?

☐ YES
☐ NO

If yes, does getting annoyed . . .

- Affect how you feel about yourself? ☐ ☐ ☐
- Play a role in your relationship(s)? ☐ ☐ ☐
- Show up in your work/school? ☐ ☐ ☐
- Impact your ability to make future plans? ☐ ☐ ☐

What are some examples of when this has happened?

How do you cope?

Share this page with . . .

☐ Family/Partner
☐ Friend
☐ Doctor
☐ Therapist/Coach/Support Group

On the other hand, do you get really annoyed when other people go off on tangents, wishing they'd hurry up and get to the point?

Brandy: Yes.

Godwin: Yes, because I already know what they're going to say. I've learned not to interrupt and tell them what they're about to say; then they change it out of spite.

Belinda: Yes, I'm impatient with others. I tend to think of what my response will be as they're speaking. As I said before, life is a chess game.

Austin: Sometimes it's comforting when people take a tangent and continue down something that interests them. I like to ask them lots of follow-up questions and stay on topics that other people aren't engaged with. I find that to be more interesting than sharing, but if someone's talking about a really boring topic that I find disengaging, then I will definitely have a hard time paying attention and will try to divert the conversation toward something more interesting. I also think that I am keeping tabs in a group conversation as to who's speaking and who's not speaking and who feels uncomfortable, and I try to throw softballs to people who are more quiet or disengaged so that they can find topics that are interesting to them and are joined into a conversation. I feel like I'm constantly trying to balance the skills for the group.

Toshi: Yes. I prefer stories that get straight to the point. If not, I miss the point and the whole story collapses for me.

Muniqui: Absolutely. I wish they would stick to the topic and get to the damn point!

Sara: Um. Yes. Wow, these questions are incredible.

Nathan: I have very little patience for anything that doesn't have a point . . . unless it interests me personally or is inherently interesting. Unfortunately, most tangents are neither (mine included).

Q 21

Do you drink coffee or other caffeine-containing substances (soda, chocolate, energy drinks) in greater quantities than most people do?

☐ YES
☐ NO

If yes, how does drinking caffeine . . .

• Affect how you feel about yourself?	☐	☐	☐
• Play a role in your relationship(s)?	☐	☐	☐
• Show up in your work/school?	☐	☐	☐
• Impact your ability to make future plans?	☐	☐	☐

When do you use caffeine and for what purpose?

How do you cope when you don't have it?

Share this page with . . .

☐ Family/Partner
☐ Friend
☐ Doctor
☐ Therapist/Coach/Support Group

Do you drink coffee or other caffeine-containing substances (soda, chocolate, energy drinks) in greater quantities than most people do?

Brandy: Yes. All the time, and it helps me focus. Caffeine will help curb a migraine.

Godwin: Yeah, I'm the same. I would literally have a coffee and my medication at the same time.

Belinda: I stopped drinking coffee two years ago to be healthier. Occasionally, I take a sip of a cola, but I just buy clear Zevia (caffeine-free) to avoid caffeine and sugar because my son is also neurodivergent. I used to drink Diet Dr. Pepper in college.

Austin: Yes, I definitely use coffee to self-medicate.

Toshi: Yes, I do. I prefer to drink coffee consciously while I'm at my desk to keep my focus steady.

Muniqui: Maybe not more than most people, but I do consume them.

Sara: Not necessarily. I'm in Seattle. But I drink a good amount.

Nathan: Definitely. A day without coffee is . . . well, I can't even guess because I wouldn't bother trying.

Q 22

Do you usually have twenty-plus tabs open on your web browser?

☐ YES
☐ NO

If yes, how does having multiple tabs open . . .			
• Affect how you feel about yourself?	☐	☐	☐
• Play a role in your relationship(s)?	☐	☐	☐
• Show up in your work/school life?	☐	☐	☐
• Impact your ability to make future plans?	☐	☐	☐

How do you feel if, by accident or intentionally, someone closes all your tabs?

Have you ever had another person make fun of you for your multiple tabs?

Share this page with . . .

☐ Family/Partner
☐ Friend
☐ Doctor
☐ Therapist/Coach/Support Group

Do you usually have twenty-plus tabs open on your web browser?

Brandy: Yes. I use my browser like a to-do list or reminder for things I want to go back to or not forget. I also found that the maximum number of tabs you can have open is 500! Shh.

Godwin: Yes, my cell phone is worse, though. There's tabs in the hundreds open in each browser. Hmm? Maybe that's why my phone is slow. I'm going to close some tabs now! Thanks for the reminder!

Belinda: Yes, I hit the maximum 500 tabs on Safari, so I use multiple browsers.

Austin: Yes! I work on lots of different devices, and each has between fifteen and twenty active tabs, documents, and projects open.

Toshi: Yes, I do. When I'm browsing, I usually open two or three browsers, and each browser has ten or more tabs open. I use three monitors, and I usually keep YouTube on in the background while I'm browsing. Sometimes, I even have more than one YouTube video playing at the same time. I've been doing this for a long time. Is this something that could be related to ADHD?

Muniqui: Absolutely, positively, yes, I do. I have up to 100 tabs open on my browser at one time.

Sara: More like a dozen.

Nathan: Eighteen at this exact moment. Actually, I keep two browsers active. The other has eight currently. So yes.

Q 23

Do you like situations involving danger and risk?

☐ YES
☐ NO

If yes, how does taking risks . . .			
• Affect how you feel about yourself?	☐	☐	☐
• Play a role in your relationship(s)?	☐	☐	☐
• Show up in your work/school?	☐	☐	☐
• Impact your ability to make future plans?	☐	☐	☐

What are some examples of when this has happened?

Do you wish you could change this about yourself?

Share this page with . . .

☐ Family/Partner
☐ Friend
☐ Doctor
☐ Therapist/Coach/Support Group

Do you like situations involving danger and risk?

Brandy: So, yeah. It depends. I'm not going to go bungee jumping, but put it that way, I might.

Godwin: Not anymore. The danger hurts if you get it wrong when you get older. It's all painful.

Belinda: I'm usually running late; luckily, I like to drive fast. If someone tailgates me, I'll slow way down or stop short. Both of those things are great for a dopamine rush.

Austin: Yes.

Toshi: I don't like risking my life, but I do like adventure. That said, I often procrastinate on things I know I need to do, pushing them further and further until I'm under pressure. When I watch myself getting that rush of tension and excitement, I sometimes wonder if I actually like risk more than I realize.

Muniqui: No.

Sara: Oh, yes. I thought I wanted to be an environmental scientist but found the tedious nature of research maddening. I figured out that I enjoy running to fires and became a journalist.

Nathan: Most of my favorite hobbies involve the possibility of an ER visit.

Q 24

Have you missed many opportunities due to procrastination?

☐ YES
☐ NO

If yes, how does procrastination . . .			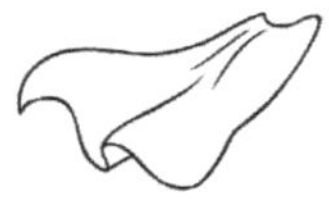
• Affect how you feel about yourself?	☐	☐	☐
• Play a role in your relationship(s)?	☐	☐	☐
• Show up in your work/school?	☐	☐	☐
• Impact your ability to make future plans?	☐	☐	☐

What are some examples of when you lost an opportunity due to procrastination?

What has worked in the past to break through procrastination?

Share this page with . . .

☐ Family/Partner
☐ Friend
☐ Doctor
☐ Therapist/Coach/Support Group

Have you missed many opportunities due to procrastination?

Brandy: Yes, I missed so many that I can't even list them all. It makes me sick sometimes when I think about the things I've missed out on because I procrastinated.

Godwin: Most definitely, yes. I'm still missing them.

Belinda: Yes, I've had to reschedule medical appointments numerous times. I missed a lot of great sales too. I've been good about staying on top of things for opportunities and deadlines. I use my calendar for everything on my iPhone.

Austin: Yes.

Toshi: Yes. The more important something is, the more I procrastinate. I can only start when it reaches the absolute last minute.I have many regrets, but there's no time to sit with it. I have to move on immediately and start working just to meet the next deadline.

Muniqui: Sadly, yes.

Sara: So many. I mean so, so many.

Nathan: Yes. There's no minute like the last minute.

Q 25

Although you may be quiet and reserved, does your mind seem to be racing most of the time?

☐ YES
☐ NO

If yes, If yes, how does a racing mind . . .

• Affect how you feel about yourself?	☐	☐	☐
• Play a role in your relationship(s)?	☐	☐	☐
• Show up in your work/school?	☐	☐	☐
• Impact your ability to make future plans?	☐	☐	☐

What are some examples of when this has happened?

How do you cope?

Share this page with . . .

☐ Family/Partner
☐ Friend
☐ Doctor
☐ Therapist/Coach/Support Group

Although you may be quiet and reserved, does your mind seem to be racing most of the time?

Brandy: My mind is constantly racing. In order to keep up with my thoughts, I make lists.

Godwin: LOL, quiet and reserved, but yes, it's hard to grab a thought!

Belinda: Yes, my mind is like the title of the movie *Everything Everywhere All at Once*. My mind only stops when I'm sleeping and not dreaming.

Austin: I noticed that my mind is racing at certain points of the day. It used to happen a lot at night before I'd go to bed, but I started listening to podcasts to redirect my thoughts to something more neutral. I also noticed that when I listened to techno music, where there's no words or no lyrics, then that gave me space to ruminate on things in my life, not always in healthy ways. I often would pick something and chew on it and then pull that situation apart many times and then feel like I couldn't stop thinking about that topic. Listening to podcasts and trying to focus on other things has been helpful, in addition to trying to give myself a mindfulness practice and listening to the thoughts and recognizing when I'm in certain modes and then trying to pull myself out through breathing and positive thinking.

Toshi: Yes. Especially when I'm driving alone—my mind is racing most of the time.

Muniqui: Yes!

Sara: I am not quiet and reserved.

Nathan: Only when I'm awake.

Are you more of a child at heart than other adults your age?

☐ YES
☐ NO

If yes, how does this childlike aspect of you . . .			
• Affect how you feel about yourself?	☐	☐	☐
• Play a role in your relationship(s)?	☐	☐	☐
• Show up in your work/school?	☐	☐	☐
• Impact your ability to make future plans?	☐	☐	☐

What are some examples of when this is a positive trait?

Is it ever a negative trait?

Share this page with . . .

☐ Family/Partner
☐ Friend
☐ Doctor
☐ Therapist/Coach/Support Group

Are you more of a child at heart than other adults your age?

Brandy: I think so.

Godwin: For my age, my middle name should be Peter Pan.

Belinda: Yes, I've always been a child at heart, even today. I was born in Peru, and the culture embraces a balanced approach: Work hard, play hard. Life is too short to be too serious.

Austin: In some ways, yes. But also compared to other people in my age group, I think I'm more mature socially. And also it depends on the day, the situation, the people, and my energy levels.

Toshi: Yes, I think so. I think and act younger than my age, and I tend to take risks when I do things or when I talk.

Muniqui: Completely. That is why I teach children.

Sara: Yes! I found out years ago that I can play with teens on their level, which made me a good leader in teen activities, long before I was a parent.

Nathan: Yes, and I intend to stay that way. My childlike curiosity is a superpower. I am endlessly fascinated by random things. And I will not stop riding the shopping cart like a scooter through the parking lot until I am physically unable to do so.

Do you often get something done extraordinarily well and have very little idea of how you did it?

☐ YES
☐ NO

If yes, how does this ability to be intuitively good at something . . .

• Affect how you feel about yourself?	☐	☐	☐
• Play a role in your relationship(s)?	☐	☐	☐
• Show up in your work/school?	☐	☐	☐
• Impact your ability to work on difficult tasks where you are not skilled?	☐	☐	☐

What are some examples of when this has happened?

How do you use it to your benefit?

Share this page with . . .

☐ Family/Partner
☐ Friend
☐ Doctor
☐ Therapist/Coach/Support Group

Do you often get something done extraordinarily well and have very little idea of how you did it?

Brandy: Yes. Sometimes, yes.

Godwin: Well, sometimes I can't even tell if I've done something extraordinarily well. I think if you have ADHD, you try a bit extra. So, you're always doing possibly more than you need to.

Belinda: I'm a big planner, so I'm intentional with setting goals. Tasks might be completed at the very last moment because of procrastination, lack of sleep caused by anxiety, or distractions due to ADHD. In any event, I know that I'll do a stellar job because of my skills in planning. However, truth be told, it's stressful to race against the clock. That's the dopamine!

Austin: Yes, definitely. I have moments where I enter a flow state if I'm very interested in a topic or have lots of energy. I can get something done without needing to eat or sleep and can work for really long periods of time, and reading, especially, used to take me a long time, and when I finished writing an essay, I'd look through it and wonder how I wrote that, and it wasn't always good, but I do sort of black out with time sometimes.

Toshi: Yes. And when I face the same kind of thing again, I end up having to rethink everything from scratch, like it's a brand-new experience.

Muniqui: Yep.

Sara: No, not really. I work hard on something and can look back at the hours it took me to get there.

Nathan: Yes.

Q 28

Do you feel huge letdowns after big events or successes more than the average person?

☐ YES
☐ NO

If yes, how does this letdown . . .			
• Affect how you feel about yourself?	☐	☐	☐
• Play a role in your relationship(s)?	☐	☐	☐
• Show up in your work/school?	☐	☐	☐
• Impact your ability to make future plans?	☐	☐	☐

What are some examples of when you have "crashed" after an event?

How do you feel at these times, and what has helped to move you through this feeling?

Share this page with . . .

☐ Family/Partner
☐ Friend
☐ Doctor
☐ Therapist/Coach/Support Group

Do you feel huge letdowns after big events or successes more than the average person?

Brandy: No, I don't think so.

Godwin: Yes, for instance, I always do my assignments last minute, and even if I get a good score on it, which should make me feel like a success, I feel let down. This is because I know I did it last minute and rushed, and I didn't put in the effort as much as I could have. I know it could have been better!

Belinda: Yes, I feel it's a bit anticlimactic after some big events or successes.

Austin: I definitely feel post-event comedown and get nostalgic about the fun that I've had and people I've met. Sometimes, after fun events, when life seems boring, I could go back to have fun! It takes me a while to balance out, maybe a day or two after a big trip or a party, before I can get back into my normal self and get past that post-event depression.

Toshi: No, I don't really feel letdowns. But sometimes I feel I shouldn't expect or want too much.

Muniqui: No.

Sara: I don't know if it's more than the average, but I certainly know the letdown feeling after an event, a trip, or a moment I've been waiting for.

Nathan: Yes. I try to be present where my feet are planted and enjoy the moment but can't help but look ahead to the next big thing.

Q 29

Are you totally amazed that so many people can't see through the facades of fake people, because you can see through them in a second?

☐ YES
☐ NO

If yes, how does this ability to read fake people . . .			
• Affect how you feel about yourself?	☐	☐	☐
• Play a role in your relationship(s)?	☐	☐	☐
• Show up in your work/school?	☐	☐	☐
• Impact your ability to make future plans?	☐	☐	☐

What are some examples of when this has happened?

How do you deal with people who hide their real selves?

Share this page with . . .

☐ Family/Partner
☐ Friend
☐ Doctor
☐ Therapist/Coach/Support Group

Are you totally amazed that so many people can't see through the facades of fake people, because you can see through them in a second?

Brandy: I'm not totally amazed, but sometimes I'm like, are people really this simple?

Godwin: I like this question, but I think it's more that people who are fake put up with other fake people because they know they're fake too. And the fake people that they have spotted also see that they're being fake too. So, it's kind of like if you won't say anything, I won't say anything.

Belinda: Yes, that's so annoying! Many people just want to maintain the status quo, or they ignore their intuition.

Austin: I do psychoanalyze people, and I feel like I can pull out trends in people's behavior. I try not to be too negative about it because everybody has their flaws and it's easy to pick people apart and focus on that, but it doesn't always happen for me, and I can sometimes get stuck in gossiping and shit-chatting and throwing shade.

Toshi: Sometimes I don't notice it, and later someone advises me, "That person was acting weird."

Muniqui: Yes.

Sara: Absolutely, positively yes.

Nathan: Yes.

Do you especially admire honesty?

☐ YES
☐ NO

If yes, how does honesty . . .

• Affect how you feel about yourself?	☐	☐	☐
• Play a role in your relationship(s)?	☐	☐	☐
• Show up in your work/school?	☐	☐	☐
• Impact your ability to make future plans?	☐	☐	☐

What are some examples of when people have lived up to your expectation of them?

How do you feel when people are dishonest?

Share this page with . . .

☐ Family/Partner
☐ Friend
☐ Doctor
☐ Therapist/Coach/Support Group

And do you especially admire honesty?

Brandy: Yes.

Godwin: I wouldn't say I especially admire it, but I do prefer it. Umm, because not many people are sincere nowadays.

Belinda: Yes, honesty is an admirable quality, especially in relationships and friendships. I prefer to know the truth, no matter how hurtful it is. I used to be brutally honest when I was younger, so I learned to have a gentler approach with the truth to not hurt anyone's feelings.

Austin: I do prefer honesty in relationships. Sometimes it's hard for me to see between the lines of what people are doing socially. I hate social chess. I really prefer when people are genuine about their intentions with people and are real. That's very important for me, and if I recognize that someone's kind of a liar or doing social chess, then it takes me a while to recalibrate how I engage with them.

Toshi: Yes. I believe honesty is the most vital thing to establish good relationships with others and for living a simple life.

Muniqui: Yes!

Sara: Yes! Dishonesty enrages me.

Nathan: Definitely. Give me an authentically imperfect interaction over a disingenuous performative act every time.

Do you especially despise hypocrisy?

☐ YES
☐ NO

If yes, how does hypocrisy . . .

• Affect how you feel about yourself?	☐	☐	☐
• Play a role in your relationship(s)?	☐	☐	☐
• Show up in your work/school?	☐	☐	☐
• Impact your ability to make future plans?	☐	☐	☐

What are some examples of when this has happened?

How do you deal with these kinds of people?

Share this page with . . .

☐ Family/Partner
☐ Friend
☐ Doctor
☐ Therapist/Coach/Support Group

Do you especially despise hypocrisy?

Brandy: Yes.

Godwin: I don't know about despising it, but it does pique my attention. In the past, I have brought it up with people, but this is like the "fake people" question. It's like you're not meant to spot hypocrisies.

Belinda: Yes, it's like a thorn in my side. My mother called it being politically correct in situations when we had to be social with fake people. She tried her best to teach me to accept it and practice that skill so as not to come off as rude.

Austin: Yes.

Toshi: Yes. I really dislike hypocrisy. Honesty is the most important value to me.

Muniqui: Yes!

Sara: Yes, it deeply bothers me.

Nathan: With a passion.

Q 32

Do you love highly stimulating environments, like chaos during emergencies, auctions, or the final moments of sporting events?

☐ YES
☐ NO

If yes, how does loving high-stimulating environments . . .

• Affect how you feel about yourself?	☐	☐	☐
• Play a role in your relationship(s)?	☐	☐	☐
• Show up in your work/school?	☐	☐	☐
• Impact your ability to enjoy calm moments?	☐	☐	☐

What are some of the high-stimulating environments you love?

How do you feel when you are in these spaces?

Share this page with . . .

☐ Family/Partner
☐ Friend
☐ Doctor
☐ Therapist/Coach/Support Group

Do you love highly stimulating environments, like chaos during emergencies, auctions, or the final moments of sporting events?

Brandy: Yes.

Godwin: Yeah, I'm good in a crisis, honestly.

Belinda: Yes, I do enjoy highly stimulating environments, like music concerts or festivals of sorts. I thrive off the positive energy. I used to work as a victim advocate at a police department. Working an assault case was an adrenaline rush; the crash after those was tough because people were hurt badly.

Austin: This really depends on if it's a topic that I'm hyperfixated on. I have some hyperfixations on feature techno art architecture, but if I'm bored by something, then if there's a lot going on, I can really tune it out and be very bored.

Toshi: Yes. They excite me a lot, and I'm able to focus more in those highly stimulating situations.

Muniqui: *Totally*, yes!

Sara: Oh, absolutely yes. Breaking news? Let's go!

Nathan: Yes. There's a beautiful simplicity to the peace that comes from having a singular focus on just this *one thing* that matters *right now*.

Q 33

Did your parents or grandparents drink too much, suffer from mental disorders, have trouble with gambling, or get into trouble with the legal system?

☐ YES
☐ NO

If yes, how does this . . .			
• Affect how you feel about yourself?	☐	☐	☐
• Play a role in your relationship(s)?	☐	☐	☐
• Show up in your work/school?	☐	☐	☐
• Impact your ability to make future plans?	☐	☐	☐

What are some examples of your parents experiencing these issues?

How do you cope during these times?

Share this page with . . .

☐ Family/Partner
☐ Friend
☐ Doctor
☐ Therapist/Coach/Support Group

Did your parents or grandparents drink too much, suffer from mental disorders, have trouble with gambling, or get into trouble with the legal system?

Brandy: Yes, my biological father with the drinking, but the rest of it, no.

Godwin: When I was older, I realized that my dad was OCD and possibly ADHD, but very, very overcompensated for. Because there wasn't any ADHD in his generation or culture.

Belinda: No, both of my parents didn't have those issues.

Austin: My dad was an alcoholic and abusive. I don't speak to him anymore. I'm pretty sure he was also ADHD, undiagnosed, probably bipolar and depressed as well.

Toshi: No, I don't think any of them had those kinds of problems.

Muniqui: No.

Sara: Drinking, yes. Gambling, yes.

Nathan: No.

Q 34

Do you often drive past the exit you were supposed to take on the highway?

☐ YES
☐ NO

If yes, how does missing an exit . . .			
• Affect how you feel about yourself?	☐	☐	☐
• Play a role in your relationship(s)?	☐	☐	☐
• Show up in your work/school?	☐	☐	☐
• Impact your ability to make future plans?	☐	☐	☐

What are some examples of when you feel like you are on autopilot?

When does this usually happen? Lack of sleep, caffeine, medication?

Share this page with . . .

☐ Family/Partner
☐ Friend
☐ Doctor
☐ Therapist/Coach/Support Group

Do you often drive past the exit you were supposed to take on the highway?

Brandy: Yes, I do it all the time, but in order to save me a lot of heartache, if I'm going twenty, thirty minutes out of my way, I'm going to put it in GPS and try to stay on track that way.

Godwin: I don't really go near highways, but even when I do, I literally always have my Waze on. Even if I know where I'm going, I just put it on.

Belinda: Yes, I tend to get distracted on the road, even with the help of GPS. It's comical at this point.

Austin: Yes, I have to keep voice navigation on so that it tells me which direction to take, and even then, sometimes I miss the directions.

Toshi: Yes. And not just a few times—many times. Navigation is very important for me when I drive.

Muniqui: Sometimes, yes.

Sara: Me? What? No, except for that one time yesterday.

Nathan: Yes.

Q 35

Are you smiling to yourself as you read these questions?

☐ YES
☐ NO

How do you feel right now?

Share this page with . . .

☐ Family/Partner
☐ Friend
☐ Doctor
☐ Therapist/Coach/Support Group

Are you smiling to yourself as you read these questions?

Brandy: Yes.

Godwin: Yes, out of compassion. No, out of frustration with the ongoingness of the thing!

Belinda: Why yes, I am. I find them to be highly relatable.

Austin: Yes, because I have done lots of personal work into my habits as a person living with ADHD, and I know lots of the symptoms line up with the general trends, and this is verifying those beliefs.

Toshi: Yes, at almost every question.

Muniqui: Yes.

Sara: Seen and surprised. I think I know so much about ADHD, but I love learning more and more.

Nathan: I am definitely smiling. I feel seen. This is therapeutic. I am trying to be as vulnerable and authentic as possible with my answers while also trying to sound cool. That last part might be the imposter syndrome talking. Okay, next question.

Are you a born debater?

☐ YES
☐ NO

If yes, how does your desire to debate . . .

• Affect how you feel about yourself	☐	☐	☐
• Play a role in your relationship(s)?	☐	☐	☐
• Show up in your work/school?	☐	☐	☐
• Impact your ability to make future plans?	☐	☐	☐

How does this trait help you?

Are there any negative aspects of this trait?

Share this page with . . .

☐ Family/Partner
☐ Friend
☐ Doctor
☐ Therapist/Coach/Support Group

Are you a born debater?

Brandy: Yes. Every conversation inevitably turns into a debate, no matter how light the topic. I can't help it.

Godwin: I believe so, but I can sometimes be overly focused on a point.

Belinda: Yes! I always questioned everything, felt the need to always defend my perspective of equality for women. I suspect it was rooted in my cultural upbringing (Latina born in the early 1970s) being told that my destiny was to be a housewife, while my brothers would be providers working outside the home.

Austin: It depends on the topic and the social group that I'm around. I definitely speak my mind when I feel comfortable; otherwise, I let people speak if I don't have the energy to go deep into it. I also think, with the polarization of the country, it's harder for me to want to engage with the tough topics, although, in my brain, I know exactly what I want to say, but sometimes I just don't think that it's worth the energy to fight people on things that they are not going to budge on. I do find it hard to structure my arguments in a logical way that's easy for people to understand. That's been something that I've really had to work hard at so that I can transfer my thoughts to other people without them getting lost or taking too many winding turns.

Toshi: I think so. I like talking about anything, and sometimes I even feel like jumping into other people's conversations.

Muniqui: Yes.

Sara: Oh my goodness, yes. Just ask my old colleagues, especially one in particular. I came to realize he was getting upset with our debates, but I had been thinking it was all in fun.

Nathan: Not unless it's purposeful. I find most debates to be the opposite—an attempt by both parties to be acknowledged as "right" without acknowledging the possibility they may not be.

Were your years of education (school, college, and beyond) marked by underachievement?

☐ YES
☐ NO

If yes, how does your underachievement . . .

• Affect how you feel about yourself?	☐	☐	☐
• Play a role in your relationship(s)?	☐	☐	☐
• Show up in your work/school?	☐	☐	☐
• Impact your ability to make future plans?	☐	☐	☐

What are some examples of when you have underachieved?

What would you like to change?

Share this page with . . .

☐ Family/Partner
☐ Friend
☐ Doctor
☐ Therapist/Coach/Support Group

Were your years of education (school, college, and beyond) marked by underachievement?

Brandy: No. I was a great student and an overachiever by nature.

Godwin: Yes, very much so, which has been challenging to enter education later in life.

Belinda: I didn't put much effort into high school because I started working at sixteen and was having too much fun on weekends, spending time with college students. I still did well. In college, I thrived, made it into two honor societies, and graduated with honors. I also got into law school twice.

Austin: I did really well in school, although that came from identifying my ADHD diagnosis and starting a medication.

Toshi: No, I don't think so. I was sometimes bored back then, but when I look back now, I realize those were happy days.

Muniqui: *Yes!*

Sara: No. I worked hard and did well. I will say that I played hard and studied hard, which left me no time for extracurriculars, and that was a strategic move.

Nathan: No.

Are you more prone than the average person to make careless mistakes?

☐ YES
☐ NO

If yes, how do careless mistakes . . .			
• Affect how you feel about yourself?	☐	☐	☐
• Play a role in your relationship(s)?	☐	☐	☐
• Show up in your work/school?	☐	☐	☐
• Impact your ability to make future plans?	☐	☐	☐

What are some examples of when careless mistakes cost you time, grades, money, or jobs?

Did you learn any tricks or tips to avoid mistakes?

Share this page with . . .

☐ Family/Partner
☐ Friend
☐ Doctor
☐ Therapist/Coach/Support Group

Are you more prone than the average person to make careless mistakes?

Brandy: Yes. Over time, I have learned to double-check my work before turning it in. I hate mistakes and misspelled words. In terms of day-to-day, I usually skip a step, miss part of an instruction, or turn the wrong way when driving!

Godwin: Yes, I think I am. But then sometimes I can be very detail-oriented.

Belinda: No, I tend to overcheck my work (thanks, ChatGPT) to avoid making more careless mistakes than the average person.

Austin: Yes.

Toshi: Yes, I think so, often. Especially when I send an email and then find a careless mistake—I feel so stupid at that moment.

Muniqui: *Yes!*

Sara: Yes, indeed. But not really in office work. It's more in clumsiness and life management.

Nathan: Yes.

Q 39

Do you feel that if other people knew "the real you," they would disapprove?

☐ YES
☐ NO

If yes, how does your mask . . .

• Affect how you feel about yourself?	☐	☐	☐
• Play a role in your relationship(s)?	☐	☐	☐
• Show up in your work/school?	☐	☐	☐
• Impact your ability to make future plans?	☐	☐	☐

Who do you worry will see behind your mask?

Who do you wish could see the real you?

Share this page with . . .

☐ Family/Partner
☐ Friend
☐ Doctor
☐ Therapist/Coach/Support Group

Do you feel that if other people knew "the real you," they would disapprove?

Brandy: No. I'm the same person all the time.

Godwin: Yes, I think so. But I don't believe that's ADHD related; it's a comorbidity.

Belinda: If other people knew the real me, I feel they would approve of me. I always seem to surprise people in one way or another. Maybe it's because I physically appear younger than my real age.

Austin: No, I actually think that the initial person that people meet is more abrasive than the real me. I have a hard time socializing.

Toshi: A part of me may not be accepted, but I'm not worried about the rest.

Muniqui: No, the opposite.

Sara: No! My attitude is *get on in here! The party is fabulous!*

Nathan: I certainly felt that way when I was younger. That has changed as I've become better acquainted with the "real me" in middle age.

Q 40

Were you the class clown?

☐ YES
☐ NO

If yes, how did being the class clown . . .

			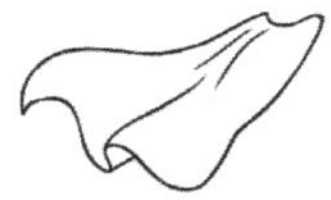
• Affect how you feel about yourself?	☐	☐	☐
• Play a role in your relationship(s)?	☐	☐	☐
• Show up in your work/school?	☐	☐	☐
• Impact your ability to make future plans?	☐	☐	☐

Are you still the clown in certain situations?

What does playing a clown help you accomplish?

Share this page with . . .

☐ Family/Partner
☐ Friend
☐ Doctor
☐ Therapist/Coach/Support Group

Were you the class clown?

Brandy: No.

Godwin: Yes, to some extent, because I was too distracted to sit still, and I like to make jokes.

Belinda: I was a class clown in some classes. I only have younger brothers, so I'd get caught up in some class hijinks. In elementary school, my academic grades were great, but my conduct grade was terrible.

Austin: Yes, but then I started medication, and that was not as big a piece of my personality, and I was more of a bookworm.

Toshi: Yes, I was. I loved making people laugh, and ever since elementary school, I was the mood-maker at family meals and gatherings.

Muniqui: No.

Sara: No, I was awkward and distracted and "only book smart."

Nathan: Yes, during my adolescent school years especially. Before going to sleep at night, I would play back the number of laughs I got and judge the quality of my day accordingly.

Did you have trouble completing your education due to problems with organization or getting to class on time?

☐ YES
☐ NO

If yes, how does this . . .

• Affect how you feel about yourself?	☐	☐	☐
• Play a role in your relationship(s)?	☐	☐	☐
• Show up in your work/school?	☐	☐	☐
• Impact your ability to make future plans?	☐	☐	☐

What are some examples of when this has happened?

Share this page with . . .

☐ Family/Partner
☐ Friend
☐ Doctor
☐ Therapist/Coach/Support Group

Did you have trouble completing your education due to problems with organization or getting to class on time?

Brandy: Yes, all of the above. Had to extend because I never took psychology and had to take it as a correspondence class. Of course, I waited to do the coursework, and I barely managed a D. It was my first and only D in my life.

Godwin: Yes, my main thing was not doing the homework. I went a year without handing in a single piece of homework for one of my lessons and somehow got away with it.

Belinda: No, I was mostly right on time for classes and was quite organized. I obtained a bachelor's degree but would like to continue my education.

Austin: I'm having trouble getting a job, but I had a really easy time with school, and I excelled, and I did really well and went to an amazing school.

Toshi: Yes. I often got things mixed up, couldn't find important memos or documents, and ended up missing deadlines.

Muniqui: Yes.

Sara: I was frequently in detention with the "bad kids" for being late, but I didn't mind. I plopped down with all my books and got so much done. It was only a couple of months ago that I realized detention was my body doubling!

Nathan: Yes, but mostly because I was more focused on partying than studying.

Do you have too many different interests/hobbies/ passions to possibly keep up with them all?

☐ YES
☐ NO

If yes, how does loving so many things . . .

• Affect how you feel about yourself?	☐	☐	☐
• Play a role in your relationship(s)?	☐	☐	☐
• Show up in your work/school?	☐	☐	☐
• Impact your ability to make future plans?	☐	☐	☐

What are some examples of when this has happened?

Is your passion in so many areas a negative trait sometimes?

Share this page with . . .

☐ Family/Partner
☐ Friend
☐ Doctor
☐ Therapist/Coach/Support Group

Do you have too many different interests/hobbies/passions to possibly keep up with them all?

Brandy: Yes. So many hobbies and interests. They can quickly take over physical space—like scrapbooking and beading—and mentally, like making lists of more things to do.

Godwin: I have many unfinished hobbies and passions. I get interested in things, and then the interest wanes.

Belinda: Yes! The rabbit hole is strong in this one. All the tabs on my Safari browser are usually maxed out. I attend webinars and sign up for clubs. I tend to double-book myself on occasion.

Austin: Yes, I have lots of interests, hobbies, and passions. I just don't have lots of time to engage with them because of my current job.

Toshi: Yes. I have so many interests that I can't follow them all.

Muniqui: Somewhat, yes.

Sara: *Yes*. And causes.

Nathan: I've never found a hobby I couldn't get obsessed with. Since becoming a full-time artist, all I want to do is spend time in the studio, so I've scaled back most of them.

Do other people comment on how hard it is to get you to stay focused, even when you want to focus?

☐ YES
☐ NO

If yes, how do their comments . . .

• Affect how you feel about yourself?	☐	☐	☐
• Play a role in your relationship(s)?	☐	☐	☐
• Show up in your work/school?	☐	☐	☐
• Impact your ability to focus on any future plans?	☐	☐	☐

What are some examples of when this has happened?

What distracts you from getting things done?

Share this page with . . .

☐ Family/Partner
☐ Friend
☐ Doctor
☐ Therapist/Coach/Support Group

Do other people comment on how hard it is to get you to stay focused, even when you want to focus?

Brandy: Yes, not always, but often. I can feel myself getting off track or losing my train of thought as it is happening.

Godwin: Not so much in my adult life. I tend to isolate myself.

Belinda: Yes, family members will point it out to me.

Austin: Yes, but I'm pretty upfront about my ADHD with people that I'm comfortable with and I own up to my traits.

Toshi: It may be true, but no one has ever told me that.

Muniqui: Yes.

Sara: Not exactly.

Nathan: Probably. I haven't really paid attention.

Q 44

Do you often make remarks that others consider odd, eccentric, or inappropriate?

☐ YES
☐ NO

If yes, how do your "off-the-wall" remarks . . .			
• Affect how you feel about yourself?	☐	☐	☐
• Play a role in your relationship(s)?	☐	☐	☐
• Show up in your work/school?	☐	☐	☐
• Impact your ability to make future plans?	☐	☐	☐

Is this sometimes a positive thing?

When or where do you find yourself making these kinds of remarks?

Share this page with . . .

☐ Family/Partner
☐ Friend
☐ Doctor
☐ Therapist/Coach/Support Group

Do you often make remarks that others consider odd, eccentric, or inappropriate?

Brandy: Yes. I've gotten better with age and experience, but basically, I went from being a loud and boisterous extrovert to an introvert who prefers to be alone, stay home, and *not* talk on the phone.

Godwin: Yes. Maybe not so much in my adult life, but when I was younger, I used to talk a lot more. So, who knows what would come out and when?

Belinda: I tend to say what's really on my mind with family or close friends, but even then, I'll need to give a warning before I say something that may be controversial.

Austin: Definitely.

Toshi: I know I can be odd or eccentric, but hopefully not inappropriate.

Muniqui: Yes.

Sara: Not often. My humor is noticeably . . . aggressive. But I think—and hopefully this is correct—that I rarely legit offend anyone.

Nathan: Yes. I try to censor them around regular people but really enjoy spending time with other weirdos where I don't have to.

Q 45

Do you prefer open shelves over drawers because if you put something in a drawer, you forget it exists?

☐ YES
☐ NO

If yes, how does forgetting things that are out of sight . . .

• Affect how you feel about yourself?	☐	☐	☐
• Play a role in your relationship(s)?	☐	☐	☐
• Show up in your work/school?	☐	☐	☐
• Impact your ability to make future plans?	☐	☐	☐

Why do open shelves help you?

What other ways have you found to "not forget" things?

Share this page with . . .

☐ Family/Partner
☐ Friend
☐ Doctor
☐ Therapist/Coach/Support Group

Do you prefer open shelves over drawers because if you put something in a drawer, you forget it exists?

Brandy: Yes. Open shelves or clear containers only. Otherwise, it basically doesn't exist.

Godwin: Out of sight, out of mind! It's not just things on shelves. It can apply to anything! But, at least, the things in my drawers don't call up asking why they haven't heard from me in a while.

Belinda: No, I have a very good memory for placement, so I prefer closed drawers. However, if something isn't written down, I forget to buy it.

Austin: I like when things have a purpose for being in my space. If I can see it, then I will use it. I'd rather get rid of something that is taking up too much space.

Toshi: Yes, very much. Putting things in drawers feels like erasing them from my memory. I'll definitely have trouble remembering where to put them. Before I put things on open shelves, I usually leave them on my large open desk with three monitors. Open shelves are the next step after my open desk.

Muniqui: No, I don't.

Sara: *No*. I am not in the open cabinet camp. No, I am not! (Really.)

Nathan: I am obsessive about organizing my space—especially my studio. I've found that the best antidote to a disorganized mind is an organized space. A place for everything and everything (occasionally) in its place.

Do you have trouble lingering with others after a meal or after you make love/have sex?

☐ YES
☐ NO

If yes, how does your need to move on to the next activity . . .

• Affect how you feel about yourself?	☐	☐	☐
• Play a role in your relationship(s)?	☐	☐	☐
• Show up in your work/school?	☐	☐	☐
• Impact your ability to make future plans?	☐	☐	☐

What are some examples of when this has happened?

Have you found a way to express your appreciation and love for the other person before you move on to the next activity?

Share this page with . . .

☐ Family/Partner
☐ Friend
☐ Doctor
☐ Therapist/Coach/Support Group

Do you have trouble lingering with others after a meal or after you make love/have sex?

Brandy: Yes.

Godwin: Yes. Because why? LOL. I've spent my energy.

Belinda: I could in the past, but now I stopped being able to linger.

Austin: Yes.

Toshi: Yes, that's true. I tend to start thinking about the next thing right away.

Muniqui: No.

Sara: Nope, not at all.

Nathan: No.

Q 47

Do you often feel an urge to hug/touch the person you are talking to, even if you barely know them, for reasons unrelated to sexual attraction?

☐ YES
☐ NO

If yes, how does this urge to connect physically . . .			
• Affect how you feel about yourself?	☐	☐	☐
• Play a role in your relationship(s)?	☐	☐	☐
• Show up in your work/school?	☐	☐	☐
• Impact your ability to make future plans?	☐	☐	☐

What are some examples of when this has happened?

How do you cope when you cannot hug someone?

Share this page with . . .

☐ Family/Partner
☐ Friend
☐ Doctor
☐ Therapist/Coach/Support Group

Do you often feel an urge to hug/touch the person you are talking to, even if you barely know them, for reasons unrelated to sexual attraction?

Brandy: Yes. I am empathetic and feel a strong urge to connect to certain people.

Godwin: Yes, sometimes, but I'm not really a tactile person. But then I can be like when you first meet them and hug them, you don't even know their name, that sort of thing,

Belinda: Yes, I tend to be a touchy-feely person with everyone.

Austin: Yes.

Toshi: Not very often. It may be because of cultural reasons.

Muniqui: Yes.

Sara: *What? Why is this question in here? Who told you?*

Nathan: No.

Q 48

Did you feel a bit out of it in school, regardless of what grades you got or how socially popular you were?

☐ YES
☐ NO

If yes, how did this feeling . . .			
• Affect how you feel about yourself?	☐	☐	☐
• Play a role in your relationship(s)?	☐	☐	☐
• Show up in your work/school?	☐	☐	☐
• Impact your ability to make future plans?	☐	☐	☐

What are some examples of when this has happened?

Why do you think you felt this way?

Share this page with . . .

☐ Family/Partner
☐ Friend
☐ Doctor
☐ Therapist/Coach/Support Group

Did you feel a bit out of it in school, regardless of what grades you got or how socially popular you were?

Brandy: No.

Godwin: Although I had many friends in school, I also knew a lot of people there. I'm not sure if I was very well liked; I think I was a bit too intense. And also, umm, you know, I'd have a different friend every week.

Belinda: Yes, I felt out of it in high school, so I started working at sixteen instead of getting involved in school activities.

Austin: Yes, but I've noticed that caffeine really helps me engage and certain foods distract me. I try to stay away from heavy carb meals while I'm doing something that requires focused attention.

Toshi: No, I never thought that way.

Muniqui: Yes.

Sara: I *was* a bit out of it in school. See awkward and distracted above.

Nathan: Yes. I would describe most of my childhood as feeling like I didn't fit in, despite some evidence to the contrary.

Are you a dreamer?

☐ YES
☐ NO

If yes, how does being a dreamer . . .		😐	
• Affect how you feel about yourself?	☐	☐	☐
• Play a role in your relationship(s)?	☐	☐	☐
• Show up in your work/school?	☐	☐	☐
• Impact your ability to make future plans?	☐	☐	☐

What are some of your dreams?

Share this page with . . .

☐ Family/Partner
☐ Friend
☐ Doctor
☐ Therapist/Coach/Support Group

Are you a dreamer?

Brandy: Yes. Both kinds. I have very vivid dreams that I can recall and sometimes rejoin. I usually know that I'm dreaming. I'm a big idea person and have always had big dreams for myself and my life.

Godwin: No, I think I'm more of a "wisher."

Belinda: Yes, I've always been a dreamer. I'd get "daydreamer" comments on report cards.

Austin: Yes, yes.

Toshi: Yes, I am. I've generated many ideas about how to get rich, and they always seem real and successful. The only thing left is actually doing them.

Muniqui: Yes.

Sara: I'm proud to be a big, ole dreamer.

Nathan: Absolutely. All big things are born from a dream.

Q 50

Do you have a sense of humor that is unusual, wacky, crazy, or otherwise out of the ordinary?

☐ YES
☐ NO

If yes, how does your sense of humor . . .			
• Affect how you feel about yourself?	☐	☐	☐
• Play a role in your relationship(s)?	☐	☐	☐
• Show up in your work/school?	☐	☐	☐
• Impact your ability to make future plans?	☐	☐	☐

What do you find funny?

Share this page with . . .

☐ Family/Partner
☐ Friend
☐ Doctor
☐ Therapist/Coach/Support Group

Do you have a sense of humor that is unusual, wacky, crazy, or otherwise out of the ordinary?

Brandy: Yes. I'm very witty. I have a dry sense of humor. I can read the room, so my humor is usually appreciated and not considered tacky—most times.

Godwin: Yeah, I think so. Umm, I tend to see the wackier side of things. Sometimes risqué.

Belinda: Yes, my sense of humor can be described as dark comedy or quirky. I've had people tell me I should be a comedian. A sitcom would be fun for me.

Austin: My sense of humor is informed by lots of nontraditional life decisions and time spent abroad.

Toshi: Yes. I've always been very good at making people laugh, and I think I'm pretty exceptional in that area.

Muniqui: Yep.

Sara: *Yes*. You might even know this by now! Yes, I do! It's on the cusp of abrasive, just right underneath. With a wink.

Nathan: Yes. I'd like to think I would have been a good stand-up comedian (but I tend to think I would have been good at a lot of things).

Do you not only think outside the box but have trouble thinking inside the box?

☐ YES
☐ NO

If yes, how does this "out of the box" thinking . . .			
• Affect how you feel about yourself?	☐	☐	☐
• Play a role in your relationship(s)?	☐	☐	☐
• Show up in your work/school?	☐	☐	☐
• Impact your ability to make future plans?	☐	☐	☐

What are some examples of when this is a positive trait?

Share this page with . . .

☐ Family/Partner
☐ Friend
☐ Doctor
☐ Therapist/Coach/Support Group

Do you not only think outside the box but have trouble thinking inside the box?

Brandy: Yes. That philosophy has gotten me into trouble. I automatically see the topic, the product, the job, and try to rework it, make it smarter, harder, and more complicated than it needs to be. Some things just need to be what they are.

Godwin: Yes, most definitely. And yes, thinking inside the box is also an issue because sometimes I can go around the houses for something that's quite simple to solve.

Belinda: Yes, I need to think about the infinite possibilities for a question/problem. I don't like restrictions when trying to problem-solve.

Austin: Yes.

Toshi: For me, being alone or in isolation matters more than whether I'm thinking inside or outside the box.

Muniqui: Yes.

Sara: I get annoyed inside the box, but I can go there.

Nathan: One hundred percent. Boxes are boring. I'd rather invent an imperfect way of doing something than follow instructions.

Q 52

☐ YES
☐ NO

If yes, how does this effect . . .			
• Affect how you feel about yourself?	☐	☐	☐
• Play a role in your relationship(s)?	☐	☐	☐
• Show up in your work/school?	☐	☐	☐
• Impact your ability to make future plans?	☐	☐	☐

What are some examples of when this has happened?

Share this page with . . .

☐ Family/Partner
☐ Friend
☐ Doctor
☐ Therapist/Coach/Support Group

Brandy: Is there a connection between a blank question right after thinking outside the box?

Godwin: ?

Belinda: Was this left blank intentionally?

Austin: ?

Toshi: ?

Muniqui: ?

Sara: This is a trick, right?

Nathan: Yes and no. Hard to say. *Wink*.

Q 53

Do you find that your thoughts go so fast that your "mental organizer" can't keep up with them?

☐ YES
☐ NO

If yes, how do racing thoughts . . .			
• Affect how you feel about yourself?	☐	☐	☐
• Play a role in your relationship(s)?	☐	☐	☐
• Show up in your work/school?	☐	☐	☐
• Impact your ability to make future plans?	☐	☐	☐

When are racing thoughts helpful?

When are racing thoughts a problem for you?

Share this page with . . .

☐ Family/Partner
☐ Friend
☐ Doctor
☐ Therapist/Coach/Support Group

Do you find that your thoughts go so fast that your "mental organizer" can't keep up with them?

Brandy: Yes. My mind never stops. When I'm brainstorming, it just overflows. The pictures run like photographs. They often outrun my writing or typing, and I have moved in a whole new direction by the time I finish writing my current sentence.

Godwin: Yes, and I think that's down to anxiety as well, but I don't have a mental organizer. It's like my room. Very messy.

Belinda: Yes, it can be overwhelming at times.

Austin: Organizing the thoughts is tough, as my mind is always racing.

Toshi: Yes, especially when my focus is near its peak.

Muniqui: Yes.

Sara: Yes. I've learned to grab a pen and paper. It helps even though many ADHDers hate the tip to "make a list."

Nathan: What's a "mental organizer"? Are we supposed to come with those? Shit.

Q 54

Were you called "hyperactive" as a child?

☐ YES
☐ NO

If yes, how did being called a hyper child . . .

• Affect how you feel about yourself?	☐	☐	☐
• Play a role in your relationship(s)?	☐	☐	☐
• Show up in your work/school?	☐	☐	☐
• Impact your ability to make future plans?	☐	☐	☐

Are you still seen as hyper as an adult?

Do you wear this term as a badge of honor or negative label?

Share this page with . . .

☐ Family/Partner
☐ Friend
☐ Doctor
☐ Therapist/Coach/Support Group

Were you called "hyperactive" as a child?

Brandy: No. I was more seen as a busybody. I was bossy and wanted things my way.

Godwin: Not specifically hyperactive. But I was called a few other names that indicated that I needed to sit down and be still.

Belinda: My dad called me "sandpiper." My mom said I was "a parrot."

Austin: Yes.

Toshi: Yes. I was very hyperactive. I would break things or injure myself, and there were times I had to be hospitalized.

Muniqui: No.

Sara: No, gosh no.

Nathan: Sometimes.

Q 55

Do you find that driving fast is a soothing experience?

☐ YES
☐ NO

If yes, how does the need to drive fast to soothe yourself . . .

• Affect how you feel about yourself?	☐	☐	☐
• Play a role in your relationship(s)?	☐	☐	☐
• Show up in your work/school?	☐	☐	☐
• Impact your ability to make future plans?	☐	☐	☐

Why does speed soothe you?

What is going on in your mind when you are driving fast?

Share this page with . . .

☐ Family/Partner
☐ Friend
☐ Doctor
☐ Therapist/Coach/Support Group

Do you find that driving fast is a soothing experience?

Brandy: Yes, if I'm the one driving.

Godwin: Yes, because I feel more focused. Driving slowly can, yes, be a bit boring.

Belinda: No, driving fast is a rush for me. It's a smooth, seamless dash, but not soothing.

Austin: No.

Toshi: No. I don't drive fast anymore. I'm not that young now, and I prefer not to.

Muniqui: Yes.

Sara: *Yes*. I love to drive fast, but more so I love to drive a stick shift up a rocky mountain road. Exhilarating.

Nathan: Sometimes.

Are you more forgiving than you imagine most other people are?

☐ YES
☐ NO

If yes, how does being a forgiving person . . .			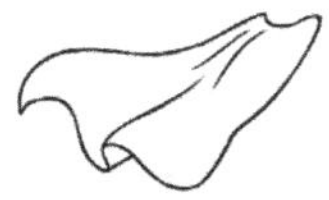
• Affect how you feel about yourself?	☐	☐	☐
• Play a role in your relationship(s)?	☐	☐	☐
• Show up in your work/school?	☐	☐	☐
• Impact your ability to stay connected to toxic people?	☐	☐	☐

Is this always a positive trait?

Would you want to be less forgiving at times or with certain people?

Share this page with . . .

☐ Family/Partner
☐ Friend
☐ Doctor
☐ Therapist/Coach/Support Group

Are you more forgiving than you imagine most other people are?

Brandy: Yes, for the most part. There are some things and some people that I will cut off and never deal with, but I will forgive the incident and be fine with cutting them out of my life. Forever.

Godwin: Yes, but I wish I were more forgiving of myself.

Belinda: I used to be too forgiving. However, once someone crosses me, personally, they no longer exist to me.

Austin: Not initially, but after deep thought, yes. If somebody's wronged me, then it takes me a really long time to process it.

Toshi: Yes, I think so. I don't cling to the past, and I don't dwell on things.

Muniqui: No.

Sara: Yes. I am.

Nathan: No.

Q 57

On the other hand, do you hate that some people take major advantage of others? And do you feel a call to stick up for them?

☐ YES
☐ NO

If yes, how does wanting to help the underdog . . .

		😐	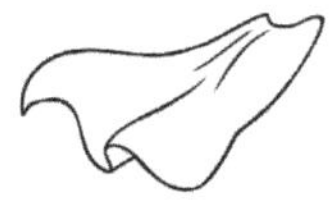
• Affect how you feel about yourself?	☐	☐	☐
• Play a role in your relationship(s)?	☐	☐	☐
• Show up in your work/school?	☐	☐	☐
• Impact your ability to make future plans?	☐	☐	☐

What are some examples of when this has happened?

How do you feel when you help someone?

Share this page with . . .

☐ Family/Partner
☐ Friend
☐ Doctor
☐ Therapist/Coach/Support Group

On the other hand, do you hate that some people take major advantage of others? And do you feel a call to stick up for them?

Brandy: Yes. I hate to see it. If I can help influence the situation in a positive way, I will try to do so. I was bullied as a kid and would not fight. My best friend would beat up all the bullies in my stead!

Godwin: Yes, I do tend to spot injustices, and yes, I can step in.

Belinda: I can't stand injustices. I've always felt a need to stick up for others. Maybe it's because one of my brothers is deaf.

Austin: Yes, definitely. I'm a person who will stick up for somebody if I feel strongly.

Toshi: Yes. I feel I have a stronger sense of justice than most people. There are times when I even think I should have been a police officer. My strong sense of justice has also gotten me into trouble sometimes.

Muniqui: Yes.

Sara: *Yes*. A call that is a constant battle to say to myself, you don't have to fight this. Maybe you should, for example, pay attention to your kid who needs you right now.

Nathan: Yes. It really bothers me to see, and when I have the opportunity to do something about it, I do.

Q 58

Do you laugh easily?

☐ YES
☐ NO

If yes, how does your ability to laugh . . .

• Affect how you feel about yourself?	☐	☐	☐
• Play a role in your relationship(s)?	☐	☐	☐
• Show up in your work/school?	☐	☐	☐
• Impact your ability to make future plans?	☐	☐	☐

What kind of shows/memes/videos/reels do you find funny?

Which do you not find funny?

Share this page with . . .

☐ Family/Partner
☐ Friend
☐ Doctor
☐ Therapist/Coach/Support Group

Do you laugh easily?

Brandy: Yes. All the time.

Godwin: Mainly at my own jokes.

Belinda: Yes, laughter is truly the best medicine. It's easy for me to laugh, to myself or with others.

Austin: Yes, if I have a social battery that's charged up.

Toshi: Yes. I love to laugh and talk, and I'm always delighted when I find someone who enjoys chatting with me.

Muniqui: Yes.

Sara: Yes!

Nathan: Very much so. I'm laughing right now. The tendency to be easily amused is one of my favorite qualities.

Do you enjoy flirting more than you imagine the average person does?

☐ YES
☐ NO

If yes, how does flirting . . .			
• Affect how you feel about yourself?	☐	☐	☐
• Play a role in your relationship(s)?	☐	☐	☐
• Show up in your work/school?	☐	☐	☐
• Impact your ability to make future plans?	☐	☐	☐

What are some times when flirting was fun?

Has flirting ever caused negative outcomes in your life?

Note to share this page with . . . .

☐ Family/Partner
☐ Friend
☐ Doctor
☐ Therapist/Coach/Support Group

Do you enjoy flirting more than you imagine the average person does?

Brandy: Yes, I used to.

Godwin: Yes, I do, but not for any particular endgame.

Belinda: I'm very friendly, which can be interpreted as flirting. I enjoy being very friendly with everyone. As far as flirting, I'm too shy to be bold about it.

Austin: It really depends. Sometimes yes, sometimes no.

Toshi: No, I'm not good at flirting. I tend to speak honestly and try to reach a mutual understanding instead.

Muniqui: I love flirting!

Sara: *Yes*. I am social!

Nathan: I don't think so. But I also don't understand what average people enjoy, so it's hard to say.

Are you slightly less coordinated than others your age?

☐ YES
☐ NO

If yes, how does being less coordinated . . .			
• Affect how you feel about yourself?	☐	☐	☐
• Play a role in your relationship(s)?	☐	☐	☐
• Show up in your work/school?	☐	☐	☐
• Impact your ability to make future plans?	☐	☐	☐

What are some examples of when you have been less coordinated?

What do you feel in this moment?

Share this page with . . .

☐ Family/Partner
☐ Friend
☐ Doctor
☐ Therapist/Coach/Support Group

Are you slightly less coordinated than others your age?

Brandy: Yes. Absolutely. I'm clumsy in general and I have balance issues due to four knee surgeries and one ankle surgery. I do warn people I walk with that I may bump into them. I love the thought of dancing but can't get my body to sync with the music and the moves at the same time. It's so hard for me.

Godwin: Yes, probably!

Belinda: I'm a bit less coordinated than others my age. I'm not the most coordinated person when it comes to syncopated steps in dancing (embarrassing for a Latina to admit); I'm much better at freestyle, feel-the-music dancing. However, I do have very fast reflexes.

Austin: No.

Toshi: Yes, a little bit—but not enough to stop me. In fact, it makes me even more active.

Muniqui: Yes.

Sara: Yes. I sometimes hurt my kids when I hug them. We all know this.

Nathan: No. I am significantly more coordinated than others my age (at least that's what I tell myself).

Q 61

Do you love it when life is going fast?

☐ YES
☐ NO

If yes, how does loving a fast-paced life . . .		😐	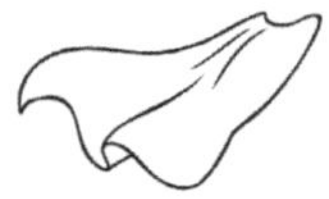
• Affect how you feel about yourself?	☐	☐	☐
• Play a role in your relationship(s)?	☐	☐	☐
• Show up in your work/school?	☐	☐	☐
• Impact your ability to make future plans?	☐	☐	☐

What are your favorite times of the year?

How do you cope when life slows down or is boring?

Share this page with . . .

☐ Family/Partner
☐ Friend
☐ Doctor
☐ Therapist/Coach/Support Group

Do you love it when life is going fast?

Brandy: Yes.

Godwin: Life is going too fast now, and I feel like I'm not doing much, so it's passing me by, so no.

Belinda: Yes, I love it when life is going fast to achieve my goals quicker. However, if I'm behind, I wish I had more than twenty-four hours per day.

Austin: No.

Toshi: Yes. Even though I tend to let my own work pile up, I really appreciate it when others respond quickly. But when someone is slow, I easily get irritated.

Muniqui: Yes.

Sara: Yes. I love it.

Nathan: I definitely have a hard time sitting still, but I try to balance my desire for intensity with a willingness to be still.

Q 62

Do you simultaneously yearn to fit in but hate to conform?

☐ YES
☐ NO

If yes, how do these conflicting desires . . .		😐	
• Affect how you feel about yourself?	☐	☐	☐
• Play a role in your relationship(s)?	☐	☐	☐
• Show up in your work/school?	☐	☐	☐
• Impact your ability to join groups?	☐	☐	☐

How do you want to fit in?

What do you hate about conforming?

Share this page with . . .

☐ Family/Partner
☐ Friend
☐ Doctor
☐ Therapist/Coach/Support Group

Do you simultaneously yearn to fit in but hate to conform?

Brandy: Yes.

Godwin: I think I yearn to fit in and do regular people things, but not just to be liked.

Belinda: No, I'm in my early fifties now, so fitting in is not as important to me. I've always had issues with conforming. I still have that teenage rebel spirit.

Austin: Yes.

Toshi: Yes. I want to fit in, but I don't want to be the same as everyone else. I prefer to be different.

Muniqui: No.

Sara: Yes. But don't we all? Is this not how everyone thinks?

Nathan: Definitely. I like the idea of fitting in but dislike the concessions that conformity requires.

Q 63

Do others complain that if you were more motivated or just tried harder, you could pay attention better?

☐ YES
☐ NO

If yes, how do these complaints . . .			
• Affect how you feel about yourself?	☐	☐	☐
• Play a role in your relationship(s)?	☐	☐	☐
• Show up in your work/school?	☐	☐	☐
• Impact your ability to make future plans?	☐	☐	☐

What do you do when someone makes these comments?

Do you wish that person could understand how it feels to have ADHD?

Share this page with . . .

☐ Family/Partner
☐ Friend
☐ Doctor
☐ Therapist/Coach/Support Group

Do others complain that if you were more motivated or just tried harder, you could pay attention better?

Brandy: Yes.

Godwin: Not particularly. I wouldn't say so.

Belinda: No, I don't believe I've ever heard that complaint.

Austin: Unsure.

Toshi: People often tell me, "Focus! Focus!" And in my mind, I always respond, "How?"

Muniqui: Yes.

Sara: No. People see me trying because I am so open.

Nathan: Yes, but I know they are incorrect.

Do you sometimes focus extraordinarily well on a task, even "hyper focus"?

☐ YES
☐ NO

If yes, how does your "hyper focus" . . .			
• Affect how you feel about yourself?	☐	☐	☐
• Play a role in your relationship(s)?	☐	☐	☐
• Show up in your work/school?	☐	☐	☐
• Impact your ability to make future plans?	☐	☐	☐

What are some examples of when your hyper focus has really helped you?

When is your hyper focus not helpful?

Share this page with . . .

☐ Family/Partner
☐ Friend
☐ Doctor
☐ Therapist/Coach/Support Group

Do you sometimes focus extraordinarily well on a task, even "hyper focus"?

Brandy: Yes. Most especially when I'm under a deadline.

Godwin: Yes, and sometimes to my detriment!

Belinda: Definitely, and it's been very helpful in college and in my career.

Austin: Yes.

Toshi: Normally, I survive by hitting hyperfocus right at the last minute. But if I could control it, I'd love to activate it earlier and finish everything at once so I can enjoy a calm, quiet deadline.

Muniqui: Yes.

Sara: Not necessarily. I've thought about this a lot, and I don't know if I do it.

Nathan: I love the hyperfocus my ADHD affords me. I wouldn't trade it for anything. Of course it's frustrating to struggle focusing on the most basic of tasks. But the ability to get into deep flow and hammer away at something that really matters for hours at a time is pure bliss. It is a superpower I believe we all can access.

Do you get frustrated because you can't make yourself hyper focus "on demand?"

☐ YES
☐ NO

If yes, how does a lack of being able to hyper focus when you want . . .

• Affect how you feel about yourself?	☐	☐	☐
• Play a role in your relationship(s)?	☐	☐	☐
• Show up in your work/school?	☐	☐	☐
• Impact your ability to finish a task?	☐	☐	☐

What are some examples of when this has happened?

Can anything help at these times?

Share this page with . . .

☐ Family/Partner
☐ Friend
☐ Doctor
☐ Therapist/Coach/Support Group

Do you get frustrated because you can't make yourself hyper focus "on demand?"

Brandy: Yes.

Godwin: I wouldn't say frustrated, but it would be nice to have a bit more control over it.

Belinda: Yes, it's frustrating to be so easily distracted or hyperactive. However, in an emergency situation, I become superfocused on demand. I'm the "fight" person when it comes to fight, flight, freeze, and fawn.

Austin: Yes.

Toshi: Yes. I basically have only two modes—on or off, with nothing in between. When I'm in the off mode, I just pretend to work while wondering how to bring my focus up.

Muniqui: Yes!

Sara: Of course. I wish I could.

Nathan: Sometimes, although I've found that habits like meditation and journaling help tremendously. To-do lists also help, simply writing down everything I think I "should" be able to accomplish in a given day (it always starts off much longer than it needs to be, as I am a chronic underestimator of how long something will take), pairing it down to the main priorities, and accepting that if nothing else gets done, that's okay.

Q 66

Are you embarrassed by how messy your car, house, bathroom, and/or bedroom is?

☐ YES
☐ NO

If yes, how does your mess . . .			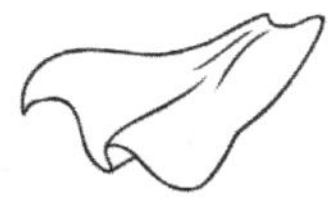
• Affect how you feel about yourself?	☐	☐	☐
• Play a role in your relationship(s)?	☐	☐	☐
• Show up in your work/school?	☐	☐	☐
• Impact your desire to entertain friends and family?	☐	☐	☐

How does having a messy car or house affect your life?

Do you avoid people or social interactions to hide your mess?

Share this page with . . .

☐ Family/Partner
☐ Friend
☐ Doctor
☐ Therapist/Coach/Support Group

Are you embarrassed by how messy your car, house, bathroom, and/or bedroom is?

Brandy: Yes, 365 days of the year.

Godwin: Because I'm pretty isolated, I don't get to see that many people, but if someone does plan to come round, that's the quickest way to get me to tidy up.

Belinda: No, because I keep my spaces clean and organized. It's part of my culture as a Latina, and it's ingrained in me. I tidy up before the housekeeper comes over to clean.

Austin: I'm a pretty clean person, but it's an active effort, and I don't stay disorganized for long periods of time. If the house is messy, it generally gets cleaned within a day or a couple hours, but I go through cycles. I'm not constantly clean, but I'm also not constantly dirty.

Toshi: Yes, very, very much. But I don't feel embarrassed in front of other ADHDers—we're the same.

Muniqui: Yes.

Sara: Absolutely killing myself with shame.

Nathan: No.

Would you have made a good salesperson?

☐ YES
☐ NO

If yes, how does your ability to sell . . .			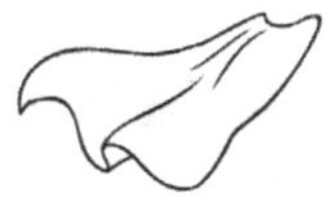
• Affect how you feel about yourself?	☐	☐	☐
• Play a role in your relationship(s)?	☐	☐	☐
• Show up in your work/school?	☐	☐	☐
• Impact your ability to make future plans?	☐	☐	☐

Where has this skill been helpful in the past?

What have you been able to accomplish or gain from your salesmanship?

Share this page with . . .

☐ Family/Partner
☐ Friend
☐ Doctor
☐ Therapist/Coach/Support Group

Would you have made a good salesperson?

Brandy: Yes. I have been a good salesperson.

Godwin: Um, this depends. I have been a good salesperson, but it depends on whether I'm following the script or not; I'm more intuitive.

Belinda: Yes, if I believed in what I was selling.

Austin: Hmmm. It depends on the product. It's very easy for me to sell something if it aligns with my interests and values, but I have a hard time selling a bad product and hate ripping people off.

Toshi: Yes. I was always a top salesperson.

Muniqui: Yes.

Sara: I would and I have. I actually talk about that: how sales isn't a bad word if it's something you're passionate about.

Nathan: I spent a number of my early working years in sales. It aligned very well with my strengths.

Would you have made a rotten accountant?

☐ YES
☐ NO

If yes, how does your poor financial skills . . .			
• Affect how you feel about yourself?	☐	☐	☐
• Play a role in your relationship(s)?	☐	☐	☐
• Show up in your work/school?	☐	☐	☐
• Impact your ability to make future plans?	☐	☐	☐

What are some examples of when keeping track of money has been hard?

What were the consequences?

Share this page with . . .

☐ Family/Partner
☐ Friend
☐ Doctor
☐ Therapist/Coach/Support Group

Would you have made a rotten accountant?

Brandy: Yes. I dropped accounting and changed my business major to communications. It was such a better fit.

Godwin: Yes, I'm not good at math or handling money.

Belinda: No, I'm very organized about receipts and paperwork, but I'd need a calculator. I'm not good with mental math computation.

Austin: No.

Toshi: Yes. I would certainly mess things up. If I worked as an accountant, it would be a nightmare for me.

Muniqui: No.

Sara: There could be no worse job for me.

Nathan: The worst. The very idea of it makes me nauseous.

Even if you don't like doing it, do you do your best work under a deadline?

☐ YES
☐ NO

If yes, how does your need for deadlines . . .

• Affect how you feel about yourself?	☐	☐	☐
• Play a role in your relationship(s)?	☐	☐	☐
• Show up in your work/school?	☐	☐	☐
• Impact your ability to finish tasks that have no deadline?	☐	☐	☐

What are some examples of when this has happened?

When is this a positive trait, and when is this a negative one?

Share this page with . . .

☐ Family/Partner
☐ Friend
☐ Doctor
☐ Therapist/Coach/Support Group

Even if you don't like doing it, do you do your best work under a deadline?

Brandy: Yes, 100 percent.

Godwin: What? Like doing this questionnaire at the last minute? Umm, yes, possibly!

Belinda: Yes, I tend to do my best work under a time crunch.

Austin: I hate time pressure, and it really takes all my effort.

Toshi: Yes. I do my best work under a deadline, because otherwise, I never start the task in the first place.

Muniqui: Yes!

Sara: Yes, but I would argue that's true for everyone. Wait. Isn't it?

Nathan: Unfortunately, yes.

Q 70

Do you find that you can get more done in twenty minutes while waiting in an airport than in six hours working in your office?

☐ YES
☐ NO

If yes, how does this type of focus . . .			
• Affect how you feel about yourself?	☐	☐	☐
• Play a role in your relationship(s)?	☐	☐	☐
• Show up in your work/school?	☐	☐	☐
• Impact your ability to make future plans?	☐	☐	☐

What are some examples of when this has happened?

When is this a positive trait, and when is this a negative one?

Share this page with . . .

☐ Family/Partner
☐ Friend
☐ Doctor
☐ Therapist/Coach/Support Group

Do you find that you can get more done in twenty minutes while waiting in an airport than in six hours working in your office?

Brandy: Yes.

Godwin: Well, I'm good in a crisis, and I like airports. I get focused in airports.

Belinda: Yes! Working in my office for six hours would be less productive due to distractions such as phone calls, coworkers, and lunch breaks. Twenty minutes in an airport is like crutch time for a deadline.

Austin: No.

Toshi: Yes. This question made me realize that I might be a terrible businessperson.

Muniqui: Yes.

Sara: *Yes*.

Nathan: Absolutely. I have a number of self-imposed rules for myself that I try to follow. My rule for flights is no entertainment or Wi-Fi unless it's an international flight of five hours or longer. The white noise, absence of distractions, and inability to do anything else is a perfect recipe for getting things done.

Do you wonder why so many people refuse to take chances?

☐ YES
☐ NO

If yes, how does your ease at taking chances . . .			
• Affect how you feel about yourself?	☐	☐	☐
• Play a role in your relationship(s)?	☐	☐	☐
• Show up in your work/school?	☐	☐	☐
• Impact your ability to make future plans?	☐	☐	☐

What are some examples of when this has happened?

When is this a positive trait, and when is this a negative one?

Note to share this page with . . . .

☐ Family/Partner
☐ Friend
☐ Doctor
☐ Therapist/Coach/Support Group

Do you wonder why so many people refuse to take chances?

Brandy: Yes. Why not?

Godwin: Not really, because I think I'm one of those people.

Belinda: Yes, and I figure that they would rather play it safe, which, to me, translates to fear. That's not living.

Austin: No.

Toshi: Because they are too clever.

Muniqui: No.

Sara: *Yes!*

Nathan: Yes. Seeing risk as a necessary component of chasing big dreams makes it difficult for me to understand those who are more inclined to play it safe.

Are you drawn to high-stimulation activities, such as fast driving, heated debates, spontaneous risks, or games of chance?

☐ YES
☐ NO

If yes, how does your need for high stimulation. . .			
• Affect how you feel about yourself?	☐	☐	☐
• Play a role in your relationship(s)?	☐	☐	☐
• Show up in your work/school?	☐	☐	☐
• Impact your ability to make future plans?	☐	☐	☐

What are some examples of when this has happened?

When is this a positive trait, and when is this a negative one?

Note to share this page with . . . .

☐ Family/Partner
☐ Friend
☐ Doctor
☐ Therapist/Coach/Support Group

Are you drawn to high-stimulation activities, such as fast driving, heated debates, spontaneous risks, or games of chance?

Brandy: Yes. I have a lead foot. It has gotten me into trouble, but I would not go skydiving.

Godwin: Not so much now, but I used to a lot. I've received numerous speeding tickets. Now that I'm older, I'm a bit more chilled. So, I appreciate things when they're slowed down or not dramatic.

Belinda: Yes! I love speed and driving around other cars like it's a race. After getting my license at eighteen, I thought it'd be cool to get into Formula 1 racing. I enjoy stimulation of all kinds. It keeps life interesting.

Austin: No.

Toshi: No. I'd rather relax and enjoy the scenery, the air, and the music. I think about many things while driving, and sometimes I even talk to myself.

Muniqui: Driving a car fast. Yes. The others, no.

Sara: Yes, yes, yes!
Nathan: Yes. The risks I take today are much more calculated than they used to be, but that's the result of consequences. Losses from gambling, a suspended driver's license for speeding, and addiction to drugs have taught me a lot.

Q 73

Do you excel in certain activities but have trouble figuring out how to make money doing them?

☐ YES
☐ NO

If yes, how does your struggles to make money . . .		😐	
• Affect how you feel about yourself?	☐	☐	☐
• Play a role in your relationship(s)?	☐	☐	☐
• Show up in your work/school?	☐	☐	☐
• Impact your ability to make future plans?	☐	☐	☐

What are some examples of when this has happened?

When is this a positive trait, and when is this a negative one?

Note to share this page with . . . .

☐ Family/Partner
☐ Friend
☐ Doctor
☐ Therapist/Coach/Support Group

Do you excel in certain activities but have trouble figuring out how to make money doing them?

Brandy: Yes. Especially my expensive hobbies.

Godwin: Ouch, this question hurts, but yes.

Belinda: Yes, I hope to be able to figure it out in the near future.

Austin: Yes.

Toshi: Yes. I can come up with many ideas for other people, but when it comes to myself, the flow of ideas sometimes stops.

Muniqui: Yes!

Sara: Not necessarily, unless you want to talk about how public radio is not lucrative.

Nathan: No. I am fortunate and grateful to have found things that do both.

Q 74

Do you have a razor-sharp memory one moment, only to be foggy and absentminded the next?

☐ YES
☐ NO

If yes, how does this . . .			
• Affect how you feel about yourself?	☐	☐	☐
• Play a role in your relationship(s)?	☐	☐	☐
• Show up in your work/school?	☐	☐	☐
• Impact your ability to be consistent?	☐	☐	☐

What are some examples of when this has happened?

When is this a positive trait, and when is this a negative one?

Note to share this page with . . . .

☐ Family/Partner
☐ Friend
☐ Doctor
☐ Therapist/Coach/Support Group

Do you have a razor-sharp memory one moment, only to be foggy and absentminded the next?

Brandy: Yes. I can remember everything from first grade but can't remember what I needed in the pantry just now.

Godwin: Again, yes, that depends. If it's related to a previous argument, then I can recall everything. But if it's day-to-day stuff, then yes, no chance.

Belinda: Yes, in the last three years, I've lost two very important loved ones. It's really caused more absent-mindedness to my usual razor-sharp memory.

Austin: Yes.

Toshi: Yes. When I decide something is not interesting, it can disappear from my memory completely. For example, I often park my car in a large parking lot, think I've memorized the location, and then find myself unable to remember it at all when I come back. I often end up wandering around looking for my car.

Muniqui: Yes.

Sara: Yes. I can still remember phone numbers from elementary school.
Nathan: Definitely.

Q 75

Do you have a million new ideas but have trouble turning them into reality?

☐ YES
☐ NO

If yes, how does your inability to turn ideas into reality . . .

• Affect how you feel about yourself?	☐	☐	☐
• Play a role in your relationship(s)?	☐	☐	☐
• Show up in your work/school?	☐	☐	☐
• Impact your ability to make future plans?	☐	☐	☐

What are some examples of when this has happened?

When is this a positive trait, and when is this a negative one?

Note to share this page with . . . .

☐ Family/Partner
☐ Friend
☐ Doctor
☐ Therapist/Coach/Support Group

Do you have a million new ideas but have trouble turning them into reality?

Brandy: Yes. And I also have a million tabs open on my internet browser. Each page represents a new idea.

Godwin: No, I have a few ideas, but I struggle to turn them into reality.

Belinda: Yes, I'm always thinking about new ideas like I'm an inventor. Turning them into reality might be easier now with social media as a conduit.

Austin: Yes.

Toshi: No. I have more ideas than I can possibly manage—that's the real problem.

Muniqui: The bane of my existence, yes.

Sara: So many ideas. So much procrastination. So many loose ends.

Nathan: I couldn't execute the ideas I have in a thousand lifetimes.

Q 76

Do you do your best work when you can be your own boss?

- ☐ YES
- ☐ NO

If yes, how does being your own boss . . .			
• Affect how you feel about yourself?	☐	☐	☐
• Play a role in your relationship(s)?	☐	☐	☐
• Show up in your work/school?	☐	☐	☐
• Impact your ability to plan for the future?	☐	☐	☐

What are some examples of when this has happened?

When is this a positive trait, and when is this a negative one?

Note to share this page with . . . .

- ☐ Family/Partner
- ☐ Friend
- ☐ Doctor
- ☐ Therapist/Coach/Support Group

Do you do your best work when you can be your own boss?

Brandy: No. But I like to have the final look on group work or projects. It's partly a control issue but also gives me some leeway with my timeline and deadlines.

Godwin: Yes, I like to work on my own. I fear comparison, but I'm the only person comparing.

Belinda: Yes, but I need to be a tough boss to stay focused.

Austin: Yes and no.

Toshi: Yes, very much. I work best when I'm my own boss. I don't need any more bosses—I want freedom.

Muniqui: No. I need a coach, manager, or teammate to help me stay focused.

Sara: No, I do not! I can't keep myself on task.

Nathan: Yes. I have worked for myself since I was a teenager. I make a terrible employee.

Q 77

Even though you may be at your best when you're your own boss, do you also benefit from having someone who can remind you to stay on track?

☐ YES
☐ NO

If yes, how does having someone to keep you on track . . .

- Affect how you feel about yourself? ☐ ☐ ☐
- Play a role in your relationship(s)? ☐ ☐ ☐
- Show up in your work/school? ☐ ☐ ☐
- Impact your ability to make future plans? ☐ ☐ ☐

What are some examples of when this has happened?

When is this a positive trait, and when is this a negative one?

Note to share this page with . . . .

☐ Family/Partner
☐ Friend
☐ Doctor
☐ Therapist/Coach/Support Group

Even though you may be at your best when you're your own boss, do you also benefit from having someone who can remind you to stay on track?

Brandy: Yes. I'm not always focused enough to actually meet the required deadlines for business on my own with no accountability.

Godwin: It depends on how they do it. Sometimes, if I'm reminded to stay on track, it can make me feel like I'm failing.

Belinda: Yes, having an accountability buddy is a very helpful thing.

Austin: Yes.

Toshi: Yes, sometimes it helps. But I hate it when people remind me too much about what to do.

Muniqui: Yes.

Sara: Ha ha. *Yep*.

Nathan: Yes.

Q 78

Do you find that you focus better amid a crisis or an emergency than when all is peaceful and calm around you?

☐ YES
☐ NO

If yes, how does your clear focus in a crisis . . .			
• Affect how you feel about yourself?	☐	☐	☐
• Play a role in your relationship(s)?	☐	☐	☐
• Show up in your work/school?	☐	☐	☐
• Impact your ability to make future plans?	☐	☐	☐

What are some examples of when this has happened?

When is this a positive trait, and when is this a negative one?

Note to share this page with . . . .

☐ Family/Partner
☐ Friend
☐ Doctor
☐ Therapist/Coach/Support Group

Do you find that you focus better amid a crisis or an emergency than when all is peaceful and calm around you?

Brandy: Yes. Absolutely. My brain goes into activate mode and I can get anything done—usually for others.

Godwin: Definitely in a crisis. If it's peaceful and calm, that's unsettling for me.

Belinda: Yes, a crisis or emergency can help me zoom in on what needs to happen ASAP. Peaceful and calm gives me time to just be and not do anything.

Austin: Yes.

Toshi: Yes. Anything unusual or any kind of trouble stimulates my adrenaline and helps me focus.

Muniqui: Yes.

Sara: *Yes!* See "breaking news" above. See . . . my friend's sliced foot in Nicaragua or my moped accident alone in Cuba. And so on.

Nathan: Definitely. Sundays are often the most difficult day of the week for me. I want to relax and be present but find it challenging to do until I've accomplished enough to feel like I've "earned the right" to do nothing.

When you attend a lecture or Zoom meeting, do you feel you pay better attention if you pace around the room or move your legs?

☐ YES
☐ NO

If yes, how does your need to move around . . .

- Affect how you feel about yourself? ☐ ☐ ☐
- Play a role in your relationship(s)? ☐ ☐ ☐
- Show up in your work/school? ☐ ☐ ☐
- Impact your ability to make future plans? ☐ ☐ ☐

What are some examples of when this has happened?

When is this a positive trait, and when is this a negative one?

Note to share this page with . . . .

☐ Family/Partner
☐ Friend
☐ Doctor
☐ Therapist/Coach/Support Group

When you attend a lecture or Zoom meeting, do you feel you pay better attention if you pace around the room or move your legs?

Brandy: No. Maybe not pacing, but I doodle to keep my focus.

Godwin: Lectures, I'm terrible at. Zoom calls, I'm not too bad at having a call in a swivel chair. The ability to move really helps me.

Belinda: I need to try that during the next Zoom call. I'm good at paying attention if the presenter is asking for input.

Austin: Yes.

Toshi: Zoom, yes. Sitting too close to the front or center is not good for me. I focus best when I'm in the back or where I can move a little.

Muniqui: Completely, yes.

Sara: Yes, I've learned to color with markers. When I walk around, I may get distracted by cleaning or reading something I pick up.

Nathan: Yes. I met my wife through work, and she noticed me walking out frequently during meetings and assumed I must be important. I definitely wasn't. I just can't sit still.

Q 80

Even though you may have noticed and assumed it was an oversight, have you forgotten by now that question fifty-two was left blank?

☐ YES
☐ NO

If yes, how does your ability to forget . . .			
• Affect how you feel about yourself?	☐	☐	☐
• Play a role in your relationship(s)?	☐	☐	☐
• Show up in your work/school?	☐	☐	☐
• Impact your ability to make future plans?	☐	☐	☐

What are some examples of when this has happened?

When is this a positive trait, and when is this a negative one?

Note to share this page with . . . .

☐ Family/Partner
☐ Friend
☐ Doctor
☐ Therapist/Coach/Support Group

Even though you may have noticed and assumed it was an oversight, have you forgotten by now that question fifty-two was left blank?

Brandy: No. It annoyed me.

Godwin: Yes, and it is funny because I have previous experience with these questions in the 128 rooms. But I did forget. So, it was pretty funny to remember that I'd forgotten.

Belinda: Yes, I thought it was intentionally left blank.

Austin: No. LOL. I deleted it in the Word doc because I thought it was a typo.

Toshi: Question fifty-two being a blank, yes, I remember it. But I thought you had forgotten it.

Muniqui: No.

Sara: *Nope*. I whipped out an email to Katherine about it before realizing this is a trick!

Nathan: Yes.

Do you sometimes become so absorbed in what you're doing that you lose track of time, meals, or your surroundings?

☐ YES
☐ NO

If yes, how does your ability to hyperfocus or be "in flow' . . .

• Affect how you feel about yourself?	☐	☐	☐
• Play a role in your relationship(s)?	☐	☐	☐
• Show up in your work/school?	☐	☐	☐
• Impact your ability to make future plans?	☐	☐	☐

When does your ability to immerse deeply in a task become a strength—and when does it cost you something?

Is the "time blindness" when you are engaged in a task something you wish you could change? And what strategies can you use to help keep track of time?

Note to share this page with . . . .

☐ Family/Partner
☐ Friend
☐ Doctor
☐ Therapist/Coach/Support Group

Do you sometimes become so absorbed in what you're doing that you lose track of time, meals, or your surroundings?

Brandy: Yes. I *often* become so absorbed or hyperfocused on what I'm doing that I lose all track of time, meals, and surroundings. My kids and I are big victims of time blindness.

Godwin: Yes, I'm doing it in real life. I'm doing another assignment due tomorrow (lastminuteagain.com), and in the back of my mind is "Oh yeah, I must reply to Katherine. It's only one question. Then I go back to assignment mode unless I get a snap out of it *ping* reminder.

Belinda: Yes, I tend to lose track of time and simply forget to eat or hydrate when I'm absorbed in something. My iPhone calendar timers are necessary for appointments. Having a water bottle reminds me to drink it. If I'm running behind (which still happens), I bring snacks for the drive. These are life hacks for most people. For me, it's a strategy that needs to be intentionally planned to work.

Austin: Absolutely. When I work for the post office, I realize that I have something called time blindness and the post office. You're required to deliver mail at very specific intervals, and it's very hard for me to meet those specific intervals because I have a hard time keeping track of time, so yeah, I do kind of get lost in what I'm doing and lose track of time easily, especially when I'm super interested in something.

Toshi: It happens to me often. Sometimes I become so absorbed that I realize I've already passed the time of an appointment. When I have an appointment, I have to set a timer before I start; otherwise, I may get too immersed and miss it or be late. The timer on my smartphone is essential. I'm grateful for my smartphone.

Muniqui: One hundred percent, absolutely, totally, this is my biggest problem. I will be doing something and look at the clock, and I do not notice the time passing. Next thing I know, I'm suddenly rushing out the door because I'm late. I thought I only spent about ten minutes. Come to find out, it's been over twenty-five minutes, thirty minutes, or an hour. I literally do not experience time passing.

Sara: All the time.

Nathan: One thousand percent. Being forced to discontinue something that's flowing for any external reason bothers the hell out of me.

Are you an entrepreneur by nature?

☐ YES
☐ NO

If yes, how does your entrepreneur spirit . . .			
• Affect how you feel about yourself?	☐	☐	☐
• Play a role in your relationship(s)?	☐	☐	☐
• Show up in your work/school?	☐	☐	☐
• Impact your ability to make future plans?	☐	☐	☐

What are some examples of when this has happened?

When is this a positive trait, and when is this a negative one?

Note to share this page with . . . .

☐ Family/Partner
☐ Friend
☐ Doctor
☐ Therapist/Coach/Support Group

Are you an entrepreneur by nature?

Brandy: Yes. I started selling "recipes" in the first grade. It only blossomed from there.

Godwin: I think in part, but not totally. I like the self-sufficient work.

Belinda: Yes, I was the kid who washed cars or sold lemonade for money.

Austin: Yes.

Toshi: Yes, I am. When I was a kid, I heard that entrepreneurs are lonely, so I thought I should become resistant to loneliness. I actually practiced being alone.

Muniqui: No.

Sara: Yes!

Nathan: Yes.

Do others comment on how creative or original you are?

☐ YES
☐ NO

If yes, how does your originality . . .

		😐	
• Affect how you feel about yourself?	☐	☐	☐
• Play a role in your relationship(s)?	☐	☐	☐
• Show up in your work/school?	☐	☐	☐
• Impact your ability to make future plans?	☐	☐	☐

What are some examples of when this has happened?

When is this a positive trait, and when is this a negative one?

Note to share this page with . . . .

☐ Family/Partner
☐ Friend
☐ Doctor
☐ Therapist/Coach/Support Group

Do others comment on how creative or original you are?

Brandy: Yes.

Godwin: Yes, they do.

Belinda: Yes, I hear more about being original than creative.

Austin: Yes.

Toshi: Yes.

Muniqui: No.

Sara: Yes, they do.

Nathan: Yes.

Q 84

Do you find that sitting in a meeting or on a Zoom call is almost always a total waste of your time and agonizing to boot?

☐ YES
☐ NO

If yes, how does your dislike of meetings/Zoom. . .			
• Affect how you feel about yourself?	☐	☐	☐
• Play a role in your relationship(s)?	☐	☐	☐
• Show up in your work/school?	☐	☐	☐
• Impact your ability to make future plans?	☐	☐	☐

What are some examples of when this has happened?

When is this a positive trait, and when is this a negative one?

Note to share this page with . . . .

☐ Family/Partner
☐ Friend
☐ Doctor
☐ Therapist/Coach/Support Group

Do you find that sitting in a meeting or on a Zoom call is almost always a total waste of your time and agonizing to boot?

Brandy: No.

Godwin: I don't really do meetings. But the Zoom calls that I do, I have to be there since I am usually the person who scheduled them, so I don't mind them.

Belinda: No, I try to get the most out of them.

Austin: No.

Toshi: If a meeting doesn't genuinely interest me, it's extremely unproductive for me. In-person meetings with no clear purpose are particularly painful. Zoom at least makes them tolerable.

Muniqui: Sometimes.

Sara: No, because I like to talk. I do find waiting to talk somewhat agonizing and meetings a bit anxiety-inducing because I do not want to dominate the conversation or speak over others.

Nathan: Obviously. If the purpose isn't clear and the delivery isn't tight, I am absolutely doing other things to keep my mind occupied.

Q 85

Are you more of a night person than a morning person?

☐ YES
☐ NO

If yes, how does being a "night owl". . .			
• Affect how you feel about yourself?	☐	☐	☐
• Play a role in your relationship(s)?	☐	☐	☐
• Show up in your work/school?	☐	☐	☐
• Impact your ability to make future plans?	☐	☐	☐

What are some examples of when this has happened?

When is this a positive trait, and when is this a negative one?

Note to share this page with . . . .

☐ Family/Partner
☐ Friend
☐ Doctor
☐ Therapist/Coach/Support Group

Are you more of a night person than a morning person?

Brandy: Yes, 100 percent.

Godwin: Most definitely.

Belinda: I've always been a night person.

Austin: I go through both phases, but they tend to be long-term habits.

Toshi: I used to be a typical night person, but now I've become a very-early-morning person.

Muniqui: Absolutely.

Sara: Yes. But it has changed as I've gotten older. Plus, working 5 a.m. jobs changed me.

Nathan: It depends on what I'm doing. When I'm in flow in the studio, I have to force myself to stop at night to make sure I get proper sleep.

Q 86

Do you sometimes say things impulsively and only later realize you may have offended someone?

☐ YES
☐ NO

If yes, how does your habit of accidentally offending people . . .

• Affect how you feel about yourself?	☐	☐	☐
• Play a role in your relationship(s)?	☐	☐	☐
• Show up in your work/school?	☐	☐	☐
• Impact your ability to make future plans?	☐	☐	☐

What are some examples of when this has happened?

When is this a positive trait, and when is this a negative one?

Note to share this page with . . . .

☐ Family/Partner
☐ Friend
☐ Doctor
☐ Therapist/Coach/Support Group

Do you sometimes say things impulsively and only later realize you may have offended someone?

Brandy: Yes. All the time.

Godwin: Not so much in my older years.

Belinda: Yes, especially family.

Austin: Yes.

Toshi: I might. I try to be careful, but I often don't notice when I've offended someone until I'm told later.

Muniqui: Yes! All the time!

Sara: Not necessarily. I think I have a particularly strong social interaction game, and I try to use it for good (activism).

Nathan: Yes. I try to consider the audience before speaking, but my assessment can be wrong at times.

Do your jokes or humorous comments sometimes get misunderstood as criticism or an insult?

☐ YES
☐ NO

If yes, how does your kind of humor . . .			
• Affect how you feel about yourself?	☐	☐	☐
• Play a role in your relationship(s)?	☐	☐	☐
• Show up in your work/school?	☐	☐	☐
• Impact your ability to make future plans?	☐	☐	☐

What are some examples of when this has happened?

When is this a positive trait, and when is this a negative one?

Note to share this page with . . . .

☐ Family/Partner
☐ Friend
☐ Doctor
☐ Therapist/Coach/Support Group

Do your jokes or humorous comments sometimes get misunderstood as criticism or an insult?

Brandy: Yes, sometimes.

Godwin: It used to be when I was younger and more sociable.

Belinda: Yes, I've spoken my mind, and it's ruffled some feathers.

Austin: Yes.

Toshi: No. I'm very careful about that.

Muniqui: Yes, all the time. I don't understand why.

Sara: They would, but I think I've learned to get it just right. I hope this is true!

Nathan: Yes (see previous question).

Do you need to set a timer when you cook so you don't forget something is on the stove or in the oven?

☐ YES
☐ NO

If yes, how does your need for a timer . . .

• Affect how you feel about yourself?	☐	☐	☐
• Play a role in your relationship(s)?	☐	☐	☐
• Show up in your work/school?	☐	☐	☐
• Impact your ability to make future plans?	☐	☐	☐

What are some examples of when this has happened?

When is this a positive trait, and when is this a negative one?

Note to share this page with . . . .

☐ Family/Partner
☐ Friend
☐ Doctor
☐ Therapist/Coach/Support Group

Do you need to set a timer when you cook so you don't forget something is on the stove or in the oven?

Brandy: Absolutely. I use timers for everything. I even have to use the oven timer when I cook because I can't hit ignore or snooze. It saves me every time.

Godwin: Let's just say, my microwave and I have a very special relationship. Sorry, oven! It's not you; it's me!

Belinda: Yes! I live my life around timers.

Austin: Cooking is very intuitive for me. It's a meditative headspace that I can hyperfocus on, so I feel pretty aware of what I'm doing while I cook. Although I'm a messy cook, and suddenly, I will look down to notice a bomb has gone off in the kitchen. But I don't burn stuff.

Toshi: Yes, I need timers, especially when I cook cup noodles. It's only three minutes after pouring hot water, but if I don't set a timer, it turns into noodles with no soup—basically garbage. For cooking, smartphone timers are vital for me.

Muniqui: Absolutely, yes.

Sara: Cooking without a timer would be impossible. There would be no reason to even try.
Nathan: Either I'm crazy (which is possible), or this question was asked earlier.

Do you usually know the point a person is getting to before they get there?

☐ YES
☐ NO

If yes, how does your ability to read a conversation . . .

• Affect how you feel about yourself?	☐	☐	☐
• Play a role in your relationship(s)?	☐	☐	☐
• Show up in your work/school?	☐	☐	☐
• Impact your ability to make future plans?	☐	☐	☐

What are some examples of when this has happened?

When is this a positive trait, and when is this a negative one?

Note to share this page with . . . .

☐ Family/Partner
☐ Friend
☐ Doctor
☐ Therapist/Coach/Support Group

Do you usually know the point a person is getting to before they get there?

Brandy: Yes, and also movie plots and books.

Godwin: Ninety-nine percent of the time.

Belinda: Yes, and it's excruciating to be patient.

Austin: Sometimes.

Toshi: Yes. I often know what they're going to say, and I answer before they finish.

Muniqui: All the damn time. I wish they would just get to the point instead of droning on when I already know what they are going to say.

Sara: Oh, goodness, yes. It's hard to wait, but I wait. I think I do, anyway.

Nathan: I usually *think* I know the point long before they get there. I try to keep my mouth shut and let them finish but am often unsuccessful.

Q 90

Do your family, friends, or partner complain that you often interrupt?

☐ YES
☐ NO

If yes, how does interrupting others . . .			
• Affect how you feel about yourself?	☐	☐	☐
• Play a role in your relationship(s)?	☐	☐	☐
• Show up in your work/school?	☐	☐	☐
• Impact your ability to make future plans?	☐	☐	☐

What are some examples of when this has happened?

When is this a positive trait, and when is this a negative one?

Note to share this page with . . . .

☐ Family/Partner
☐ Friend
☐ Doctor
☐ Therapist/Coach/Support Group

Do your family, friends, or partner complain that you often interrupt?

Brandy: Yes.

Godwin: Not so much anymore.

Belinda: Yes, family members tell me all the time.

Austin: It's something I worked on a lot.

Toshi: Yes, but not at the moment. I'm still working on getting better at this.

Muniqui: Yes.

Sara: Yes, but I've been working on this for years. I bite my tongue (literally) and silently scream to myself, "*Listen!*" I think it's working.

Nathan: Yes. My wife has accurately pointed out that while I have a very low tolerance for being interrupted, I am more than willing to interrupt others.

Are you more energetic than other people your age?

☐ YES
☐ NO

If yes, how does your extra energy . . .

• Affect how you feel about yourself?	☐	☐	☐
• Play a role in your relationship(s)?	☐	☐	☐
• Show up in your work/school?	☐	☐	☐
• Impact your ability to make future plans?	☐	☐	☐

What are some examples of when this has happened?

When is this a positive trait, and when is this a negative one?

Note to share this page with . . . .

☐ Family/Partner
☐ Friend
☐ Doctor
☐ Therapist/Coach/Support Group

Are you more energetic than other people your age?

Brandy: Yes.

Godwin: Mentally, I think so. But physically, I've gone a bit sedentary. However, I am quite energetic. When I need to, I can still leap up a flight of stairs.

Belinda: Oh yes, I'm like the Energizer Bunny compared to others my age.

Austin: Yes and no. Depends on where my head is at. Fluctuates a lot.

Toshi: I think so. I'm still energetic enough to seriously consider living in New York.

Muniqui: Yes.

Sara: *Yes!* I never attributed that to my ADHD. Hmm.

Nathan: Yes.

Q 92

Are you now or have you ever been concerned that you drink too much alcohol?

☐ YES
☐ NO

If yes, how does your use of alcohol . . .			
• Affect how you feel about yourself?	☐	☐	☐
• Play a role in your relationship(s)?	☐	☐	☐
• Show up in your work/school?	☐	☐	☐
• Impact your ability to make future plans?	☐	☐	☐

What are some examples of when this has happened?

When is this a positive trait, and when is this a negative one?

Note to share this page with . . . .

☐ Family/Partner
☐ Friend
☐ Doctor
☐ Therapist/Coach/Support Group

Are you now or have you ever been concerned that you drink too much alcohol?

Brandy: Yes. When I was younger. I stopped cold turkey.

Godwin: "Never Too Much," to quote Luther Vandross.

Belinda: No concerns about ever drinking too much alcohol.

Austin: No.

Toshi: I don't drink alcohol.

Muniqui: No, never liked it. Don't understand why anyone likes or drinks alcohol.

Sara: Definitely not now, but I drank a lot in my twenties.

Nathan: Yes. I used every substance I could get my hands on, with meth amphetamine being my end-of-the-road drug of choice. I have been sober and in recovery since 2002.

Q 93

Do you now or did you ever vape or smoke cigarettes?

☐ YES
☐ NO

If yes, how does your smoking . . .			
• Affect how you feel about yourself?	☐	☐	☐
• Play a role in your relationship(s)?	☐	☐	☐
• Show up in your work/school?	☐	☐	☐
• Impact your ability to make future plans?	☐	☐	☐

What are some examples of when this has happened?

When is this a positive trait, and when is this a negative one?

Note to share this page with . . . .

☐ Family/Partner
☐ Friend
☐ Doctor
☐ Therapist/Coach/Support Group

Do you now or did you ever vape or smoke cigarettes?

Brandy: No. But I have smoked hookah.

Godwin: Yes, and yes.

Belinda: Yes, I've smoked socially as a young adult. I vaped medical marijuana in my forties after a bad car accident.

Austin: Yes, during COVID. That was an exception though. I feel like I get a pass for that.

Toshi: I used to smoke until I was forty, and then I quit.

Muniqui: No.

Sara: I socially smoked in my twenties, like most everyone I knew, to the point where if I was in a bar, I was smoking. But I was lucky to be able to quit whenever I wanted.

Nathan: No.

Are you a bit of a rebel?

☐ YES
☐ NO

If yes, how does being a rebel. . .		😐	
• Affect how you feel about yourself?	☐	☐	☐
• Play a role in your relationship(s)?	☐	☐	☐
• Show up in your work/school?	☐	☐	☐
• Impact your ability to make future plans?	☐	☐	☐

What are some examples of when this has happened?

When is this a positive trait, and when is this a negative one?

Note to share this page with . . . .

☐ Family/Partner
☐ Friend
☐ Doctor
☐ Therapist/Coach/Support Group

Are you a bit of a rebel?

Brandy: Yes. Aren't we all?

Godwin: Not anymore.

Belinda: Yes, I've always been a rebel. I don't look like a rebel, but looks are deceiving.

Austin: Yes. And an advocate.

Toshi: Yes.

Muniqui: A little, but not much.

Sara: I would definitely say yes to this.

Nathan: Yes. The idea of following the rules hurts my heart.

Even though you may be a natural rebel, have you found yourself working for someone or in a relationship with someone who wants you to conform?

☐ YES
☐ NO

If yes, how does the request to conform . . .			
• Affect how you feel about yourself?	☐	☐	☐
• Play a role in your relationship(s)?	☐	☐	☐
• Show up in your work/school?	☐	☐	☐
• Impact your ability to make future plans?	☐	☐	☐

What are some examples of when this has happened?

When is this a positive trait, and when is this a negative one?

Note to share this page with . . . .

☐ Family/Partner
☐ Friend
☐ Doctor
☐ Therapist/Coach/Support Group

Even though you may be a natural rebel, have you found yourself working for someone or in a relationship with someone who wants you to conform?

Brandy: Yes.

Godwin: I wouldn't say conform but be more consistent.

Belinda: Yes, I was in a long-term relationship with someone who wanted me to conform to their family's lifestyle just as much as he did. It was boring and exhausting!

Austin: Yes.

Toshi: I can't work under someone like that. I was a job quitter—and I'm divorced as well.

Muniqui: Yes.

Sara: Relationship: not necessarily, no. Work: yes.

Nathan: Yes, but not for very long. *Smile*.

Q 96

In romance, have you often made the mistake of dating, living with, or marrying someone who belittles you, reprimands you, and tries to control you?

☐ YES
☐ NO

If yes, how does having a controlling partner . . .

• Affect how you feel about yourself?	☐	☐	☐
• Play a role in your relationship(s)?	☐	☐	☐
• Show up in your work/school?	☐	☐	☐
• Impact your ability to make future plans?	☐	☐	☐

What are some examples of when this has happened?

When is this a positive trait, and when is this a negative one?

Note to share this page with . . . .

☐ Family/Partner
☐ Friend
☐ Doctor
☐ Therapist/Coach/Support Group

In romance, have you often made the mistake of dating, living with, or marrying someone who belittles you, reprimands you, and tries to control you?

Brandy: Yes. Several times.

Godwin: I think I have, but then, I was uncertain of myself; I wasn't really sure if my intuition was correct. I was always wrong. And I could never find them wrong, even though I thought they were at times.

Belinda: Yes, I have experienced being belittled, reprimanded, and attempts to control me.

Austin: Yes.

Toshi: No, I haven't.

Muniqui: Yes.

Sara: Yes. Sad face.

Nathan: No.

Q 97

Do others see more good and value in you than you do?

- ☐ YES
- ☐ NO

If yes, how do other people's more favorable opinions of you . . .

• Affect how you feel about yourself?	☐	☐	☐
• Play a role in your relationship(s)?	☐	☐	☐
• Show up in your work/school?	☐	☐	☐
• Impact your ability to make future plans?	☐	☐	☐

What are some examples of when this has happened?

When is this a positive trait, and when is this a negative one?

Note to share this page with . . . .

- ☐ Family/Partner
- ☐ Friend
- ☐ Doctor
- ☐ Therapist/Coach/Support Group

Do others see more good and value in you than you do?

Brandy: No.

Godwin: Yes. I think so.

Belinda: Yes, during my divorce, many friends have been vocal about how I was too good for my ex-husband.

Austin: Yes.

Toshi: I'm not sure if others value me more than I value myself.

Muniqui: No.

Sara: No. I'm so lucky that I can say I see and appreciate my good traits.

Nathan: In some cases, yes, but working a program of recovery has taught me to love and accept myself for who I am.

Q 98

Do you find that your partner has to do most of the organizing and planning?

☐ YES
☐ NO

If yes, how does this . . .			
• Affect how you feel about yourself?	☐	☐	☐
• Play a role in your relationship(s)?	☐	☐	☐
• Show up in your work/school?	☐	☐	☐
• Impact your ability to make future plans?	☐	☐	☐

What are some examples of when this has happened?

When is this a positive trait, and when is this a negative one?

Note to share this page with . . . .

☐ Family/Partner
☐ Friend
☐ Doctor
☐ Therapist/Coach/Support Group

Do you find that your partner has to do most of the organizing and planning?

Brandy: Yes. I try but get bogged down by making everything too complicated and/or extravagant. Sometimes less is more.

Godwin: I am single.

Belinda: No, we both liked to plan and I was the organizer.

Austin: Yes and no. I really have to advocate for the things I want to do and get annoyed when they don't happen.

Toshi: Yes, she does. I'm not good at organizing or planning, so I usually help by doing the shopping and the heavy work.

Muniqui: One thousand percent, yes!

Sara: Good god, no. I can only dream. This is a reference to an ex-partner.

Nathan: No.

Q 99

Does your partner resent how much they have to do for you to be in a relationship with you?

- ☐ YES
- ☐ NO

If yes, how does the strain on your partner. . .			
• Affect how you feel about yourself?	☐	☐	☐
• Play a role in your relationship(s)?	☐	☐	☐
• Show up in your work/school?	☐	☐	☐
• Impact your ability to make future plans?	☐	☐	☐

What are some examples of when this has happened?

When is this a positive trait, and when is this a negative one?

Note to share this page with . . . .

- ☐ Family/Partner
- ☐ Friend
- ☐ Doctor
- ☐ Therapist/Coach/Support Group

Does your partner resent how much they have to do for you to be in a relationship with you?

Brandy: Yes.

Godwin: In the past, I think it has been a topic of conversation.

Belinda: No, because I was a stay-at-home parent and took care of the finances.

Austin: Yes.

Toshi: Yes. She does all the housework that I can't manage, and it would be natural for her to feel some resentment.

Muniqui: One million percent, yes.

Sara: *No*. I did it all.

Nathan: Probably sometimes, although thankfully, she is very generous and understanding of my limitations and shortcomings.

Does your partner often tell you how much they care about you but also that they are going to leave you unless you get your act together?

☐ YES
☐ NO

If yes, how does your partner's care but threat of ultimatum . . .

• Affect how you feel about yourself?	☐	☐	☐
• Play a role in your relationship(s)?	☐	☐	☐
• Show up in your work/school?	☐	☐	☐
• Impact your ability to make future plans?	☐	☐	☐

What are some examples of when this has happened?

When is this a positive trait, and when is this a negative one?

Note to share this page with . . . .

☐ Family/Partner
☐ Friend
☐ Doctor
☐ Therapist/Coach/Support Group

Does your partner often tell you how much they care about you but also that they are going to leave you unless you get your act together?

Brandy: Yes.

Godwin: I am single.

Belinda: No, because I had my act together and helped keep him organized.

Austin: Not sure it's that severe.

Toshi: Yes, she did—and I said the same to her.

Muniqui: She doesn't tell me she is going to leave me, but I know she thinks about it.

Sara: No. I'm the one with my act together.

Nathan: No.

Q 101

Has intimacy and/or sex declined due to emotional conflicts with your partner?

☐ YES
☐ NO

If yes, how does the decline in intimacy and/or sex . . .

- Affect how you feel about yourself? ☐ ☐ ☐
- Play a role in your relationship(s)? ☐ ☐ ☐
- Show up in your work/school? ☐ ☐ ☐
- Impact your ability to make future plans? ☐ ☐ ☐

What are some examples of when this has happened?

When is this a positive trait, and when is this a negative one?

Note to share this page with . . . .

☐ Family/Partner
☐ Friend
☐ Doctor
☐ Therapist/Coach/Support Group

Has intimacy and/or sex declined due to emotional conflicts with your partner?

Brandy: Yes.

Godwin: I think it's declined due to a lack of partners. Thanks for the reminder!

Belinda: Yes, but makeup sex can be a great thing.

Austin: Yes.

Toshi: I think so.

Muniqui: Sadly, yes.

Sara: Yes, when I was married.

Nathan: Yes.

Do you find that you have trouble sustaining attention when you are sharing intimate moments/having sex, even though you are aroused and interested?

☐ YES
☐ NO

If yes, how does your lack of attention . . .			
• Affect how you feel about yourself?	☐	☐	☐
• Play a role in your relationship(s)?	☐	☐	☐
• Show up in your work/school?	☐	☐	☐
• Impact your ability to make future plans?	☐	☐	☐

What are some examples of when this has happened?

When is this a positive trait, and when is this a negative one?

Note to share this page with . . . .

☐ Family/Partner
☐ Friend
☐ Doctor
☐ Therapist/Coach/Support Group

Do you find that you have trouble sustaining attention when you are sharing intimate moments/having sex, even though you are aroused and interested?

Brandy: Yes. It's so irritating and causes a lot of problems. My face tells all.

Godwin: Anonymously, yes. That's happened.

Belinda: Yes, during sex, I'd run through my to-do list for the next day.

Austin: No.

Toshi: Yes, I do.

Muniqui: Not really.

Sara: Yes, sometimes.

Nathan: No.

Q 103

Do you think you have a higher level of sexual interest, drive, and curiosity than others your age?

☐ YES
☐ NO

If yes, how does this higher level . . .			
• Affect how you feel about yourself?	☐	☐	☐
• Play a role in your relationship(s)?	☐	☐	☐
• Show up in your work/school?	☐	☐	☐
• Impact your ability to make future plans?	☐	☐	☐

What are some examples of when this has happened?

When is this a positive trait, and when is this a negative one?

Note to share this page with . . . .

☐ Family/Partner
☐ Friend
☐ Doctor
☐ Therapist/Coach/Support Group

Do you think you have a higher level of sexual interest, drive, and curiosity than others your age?

Brandy: No.

Godwin: I don't know. I haven't asked.

Belinda: Yes, I've always had a higher level of sexual interest, drive and curiosity than others my age, especially the drive.

Austin: Yes.

Toshi: I might be.

Muniqui: Not really.

Sara: Yes.

Nathan: Possibly. Difficult to say.

Are you thinking about other things in the back of your mind as you read these questions?

☐ YES
☐ NO

If yes, how does your mind on two different tasks . . .			
• Affect how you feel about yourself?	☐	☐	☐
• Play a role in your relationship(s)?	☐	☐	☐
• Show up in your work/school?	☐	☐	☐
• Impact your ability to make future plans?	☐	☐	☐

What are some examples of when this has happened?

When is this a positive trait, and when is this a negative one?

Note to share this page with . . . .

☐ Family/Partner
☐ Friend
☐ Doctor
☐ Therapist/Coach/Support Group

Are you thinking about other things in the back of your mind as you read these questions?

Brandy: Yes. So many.

Godwin: Of course . . .

Belinda: I'm thinking about a few things as I go through these questions.

Austin: Yes.

Toshi: Yes. I'm thinking about how far these questions will go.

Muniqui: Yes.

Sara: Aren't we all doing that all the time? I thought we were. Anyway, yes.

Nathan: I mean, yeah. The list of activities where that wouldn't apply is very short.

As you are finishing this quiz, is your mind already searching for what would be interesting/fun to do next—and avoiding some less pleasant task you should do?

☐ YES
☐ NO

If yes, how does this distraction . . .			
• Affect how you feel about yourself?	☐	☐	☐
• Play a role in your relationship(s)?	☐	☐	☐
• Show up in your work/school?	☐	☐	☐
• Impact your ability to make future plans?	☐	☐	☐

What are some examples of when this has happened?

When is this a positive trait, and when is this a negative one?

Note to share this page with . . . .

☐ Family/Partner
☐ Friend
☐ Doctor
☐ Therapist/Coach/Support Group

As you are finishing this quiz, is your mind already searching for what would be interesting/fun to do next—and avoiding some less pleasant task you should do?

Brandy: Yes.

Godwin: Probably, definitely.

Belinda: No, I'm going to try to go to sleep after this quiz.

Austin: Yes.

Toshi: I'm thinking about both—what I'm supposed to do next and what I'm not supposed to do.

Muniqui: No.

Sara: Yes. Watch a movie instead of clean the living room.

Nathan: Yes. I have about fifty-seven things in mind, and time for maybe three?

Do you carry anger and frustration that comes out too easily or at the wrong times?

☐ YES
☐ NO

If yes, how does your anger and frustration . . .			
• Affect how you feel about yourself?	☐	☐	☐
• Play a role in your relationship(s)?	☐	☐	☐
• Show up in your work/school?	☐	☐	☐
• Impact your ability to make future plans?	☐	☐	☐

What are some examples of when this has happened?

When is this a positive trait, and when is this a negative one?

Note to share this page with . . . .

☐ Family/Partner
☐ Friend
☐ Doctor
☐ Therapist/Coach/Support Group

Do you carry anger and frustration that comes out too easily or at the wrong times?

Brandy: Yes. Sometimes.

Godwin: I wouldn't say I carry it, but I can be short-tempered at times. However, that's probably because I've given the issue thought and I know I'm right. And it's frustrating to have to repeat myself, even though I haven't said anything to the person.

Belinda: Yes, the only anger and frustration that I carry can come out at the wrong time.

Austin: Yes.

Toshi: Yes, I do. And I can usually tell when it's about to explode or not.

Muniqui: No.

Sara: Yes, I feel ragey at times, and I show it.

Nathan: Yes, although I continue to work on myself and with others to identify and work through resentments before they come out sideways.

Do you feel more mentally focused after you exercise?

☐ YES
☐ NO

If yes, how does your exercise . . .			
• Affect how you feel about yourself?	☐	☐	☐
• Play a role in your relationship(s)?	☐	☐	☐
• Show up in your work/school?	☐	☐	☐
• Impact your ability to make future plans?	☐	☐	☐

What are some examples of when this has happened?

When is this a positive trait, and when is this a negative one?

Note to share this page with . . . .

☐ Family/Partner
☐ Friend
☐ Doctor
☐ Therapist/Coach/Support Group

Do you feel more mentally focused after you exercise?

Brandy: Yes.

Godwin: I'm not too sure.

Belinda: Yes, exercise is my Adderall.

Austin: Yes.

Toshi: Yes, I do.

Muniqui: Yes.

Sara: Yes, definitely.

Nathan: Yes. I have found that consistently training hard has just as much mental and emotional benefit than just health and fitness (if not more).

Q 108

Do you sometimes have trouble putting your thoughts into words?

☐ YES
☐ NO

If yes, how does having trouble putting your thoughts into words . . .

• Affect how you feel about yourself?	☐	☐	☐
• Play a role in your relationship(s)?	☐	☐	☐
• Show up in your work/school?	☐	☐	☐
• Impact your ability to make future plans?	☐	☐	☐

What are some examples of when this has happened?

When is this a positive trait, and when is this a negative one?

Note to share this page with . . . .

☐ Family/Partner
☐ Friend
☐ Doctor
☐ Therapist/Coach/Support Group

Do you sometimes have trouble putting your thoughts into words?

Brandy: Yes. Sometimes.

Godwin: Not really. I'm quite articulate.

Belinda: Yes, on occasion, when I'm frustrated. It also happens more when I speak in Spanish.

Austin: When the ADHD fog is heavy, yes, but when I'm comfy and rested, no.

Toshi: Yes, I have.

Muniqui: Yes, especially when writing.

Sara: No, I'm quite verbal.

Nathan: I don't have too much trouble putting thoughts into words, but putting feelings into words can be challenging for me.

Q 109

Has your partner ever told you that communicating with you can be difficult?

☐ YES
☐ NO

If yes, how do your partner's comments . . .		😐	
• Affect how you feel about yourself?	☐	☐	☐
• Play a role in your relationship(s)?	☐	☐	☐
• Show up in your work/school?	☐	☐	☐
• Impact your ability to make future plans?	☐	☐	☐

Does your partner say that conversations with you can feel confusing, overwhelming, or hard to follow at times?

When is this a positive trait, and when is this a negative one?

Note to share this page with . . ..

☐ Family/Partner
☐ Friend
☐ Doctor
☐ Therapist/Coach/Support Group

Has your partner ever told you that communicating with you can be difficult?

Brandy: Yes. Daily.

Godwin: Again with the partner questions. Are you trying to upset me? LOL.

Belinda: Yes, my ex-husband has told me that he feels like he's "talking to a child."

Austin: Unsure.

Toshi: Yes, I think she does. But I believe every couple has communication difficulties. No?

Muniqui: No.

Sara: No. Gosh, no.

Nathan: Yes, and I am certain that it is.

Q 110

Are you dyslexic or a very slow reader?

☐ YES
☐ NO

If yes, how does your slow reading . . .

• Affect how you feel about yourself?	☐	☐	☐
• Play a role in your relationship(s)?	☐	☐	☐
• Show up in your work/school?	☐	☐	☐
• Impact your ability to make future plans?	☐	☐	☐

What are some examples of when this has happened?

When is this a positive trait, and when is this a negative one?

Note to share this page with . . . .

☐ Family/Partner
☐ Friend
☐ Doctor
☐ Therapist/Coach/Support Group

Are you dyslexic or a very slow reader?

Brandy: No.

Godwin: No. I'm a fast reader, which is probably not ideal for retaining details.

Belinda: No, I'm not dyslexic. I can read very quickly.

Austin: Yes. But I started listening to audiobooks.

Toshi: I don't think so, but I do have difficulty focusing.

Muniqui: I think I have become a slower reader.

Sara: No, I'm not.

Nathan: No.

Do you waste vast quantities of time roaming the internet, sending and receiving emails, playing electronic games, and otherwise diverting yourself from what you originally sat down at your computer to do?

☐ YES
☐ NO

If yes, how does wasting time . . .

• Affect how you feel about yourself?	☐	☐	☐
• Play a role in your relationship(s)?	☐	☐	☐
• Show up in your work/school?	☐	☐	☐
• Impact your ability to make future plans?	☐	☐	☐

What are some examples of when this has happened?

When is this a positive trait, and when is this a negative one?

Note to share this page with . . . .

☐ Family/Partner
☐ Friend
☐ Doctor
☐ Therapist/Coach/Support Group

Do you waste vast quantities of time roaming the internet, sending and receiving emails, playing electronic games, and otherwise diverting yourself from what you originally sat down at your computer to do?

Brandy: Yes. That's why I'm rushing to complete this quiz.

Godwin: Yes, all the time. I have major avoidance issues.

Belinda: Yes, I do all of the above, and I really wish that I wouldn't.

Austin: Yes.

Toshi: Yes, I have. Especially when I'm researching something on a search engine, I get hooked by other interesting things on the web. Then I lose my original target and start following whatever grabs my attention.

Muniqui: Sadly, yes.

Sara: Yes, all the time. But I have methods for it. Thanks, Focusmate and Pomodoro.

Nathan: Affirmative.

Do you love children but also get bored trying to read to them or play games with them?

☐ YES
☐ NO

If yes, how does your boredom . . .

• Affect how you feel about yourself?	☐	☐	☐
• Play a role in your relationship(s)?	☐	☐	☐
• Show up in your work/school?	☐	☐	☐
• Impact your ability to make future plans?	☐	☐	☐

What are some examples of when this has happened?

When is this a positive trait, and when is this a negative one?

Note to share this page with . . . .

☐ Family/Partner
☐ Friend
☐ Doctor
☐ Therapist/Coach/Support Group

Do you love children but also get bored trying to read to them or play games with them?

Brandy: No.

Godwin: No. I enjoyed playing with kids when I knew kids.

Belinda: No, because I used to work with children. You won't get bored if you allow yourself to become a child again. To keep things fresh, I let the kids lead the way.

Austin: Yes.

Toshi: Yes, I do. But I get bored earlier than the children.

Muniqui: Actually, no. I love to do that with children.

Sara: No, I feel like I can get into their games like a kid. I know other parents struggle with this, but that hasn't been tough for me.

Nathan: I wouldn't call it boredom. I cannot recall the last time I was bored. I'd say it's more of a frustration with attention span—both theirs and my own.

Q 113

Do you feel that your life could be much, much better if only you could make one major change or breakthrough . . . but you don't know what it is?

☐ YES
☐ NO

If yes, how does not being able to figure out how to change your life . . .

• Affect how you feel about yourself?	☐	☐	☐
• Play a role in your relationship(s)?	☐	☐	☐
• Show up in your work/school?	☐	☐	☐
• Impact your ability to make future plans?	☐	☐	☐

What are some examples of when this has happened?

When is this a positive trait, and when is this a negative one?

Note to share this page with . . . .

☐ Family/Partner
☐ Friend
☐ Doctor
☐ Therapist/Coach/Support Group

Do you feel that your life could be much, much better if only you could make one major change or breakthrough . . . but you don't know what it is?

Brandy: Yes.

Godwin: Yes, I may know what it is, but I haven't done it. I'm not sure if it would make my life better.

Belinda: No and yes to this question. My life is pretty good. There's no "if only"; it's *when* I make the change or breakthrough. The best part is that I finally know what it is, thanks to my therapist.

Austin: Yes, career.

Toshi: My life has already changed, so now I know how to create change. What I'm not always sure about is when the best timing is.

Muniqui: All the damn time.

Sara: No. I try to live in the moment and without regrets. I'm grateful I've done so much that I wanted to do.

Nathan: No.

Is your idea of a perfect party to arrive, have a drink, eat some food, talk to one or two friends, and go home with as little social interaction as possible?

☐ YES
☐ NO

If yes, how does your limited social battery . . .			
• Affect how you feel about yourself?	☐	☐	☐
• Play a role in your relationship(s)?	☐	☐	☐
• Show up in your work/school?	☐	☐	☐
• Impact your ability to make future plans?	☐	☐	☐

What are some examples of when this has happened?

When is this a positive trait, and when is this a negative one?

Note to share this page with . . . .

☐ Family/Partner
☐ Friend
☐ Doctor
☐ Therapist/Coach/Support Group

Is your idea of a perfect party to arrive, have a drink, eat some food, talk to one or two friends, and go home with as little social interaction as possible?

Brandy: No.

Godwin: Yeah. There comes a point in the evening where I am mentally tired and want to check out, and the long goodbyes aren't great.

Belinda: No, I enjoy taking my time at dinner parties. I arrive fashionably and end up staying a bit longer to help out the hostess, with cleanup, if needed.

Austin: Hmm, depends on the people and the conversation topics. My partner loves dinner parties, but I think they are a chore.

Toshi: No. My idea of a perfect party is making everyone laugh, helping everyone enjoy themselves, and then going home happily.

Muniqui: Not at all.

Sara: No! I have the hardest time not being the last one there.

Nathan: My idea of a perfect party is usually finding a way to not go at all.

Q 115

Do you sometimes smile in a conversation in hopes that it will be a sufficient contribution because you have totally lost track of what is being talked about?

☐ YES
☐ NO

If yes, how does losing track of what someone is saying. . .

			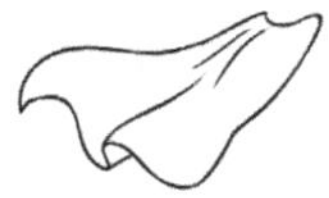
• Affect how you feel about yourself?	☐	☐	☐
• Play a role in your relationship(s)?	☐	☐	☐
• Show up in your work/school?	☐	☐	☐
• Impact your ability to make future plans?	☐	☐	☐

What are some examples of when this has happened?

When is this a positive trait, and when is this a negative one?

Note to share this page with . . . .

☐ Family/Partner
☐ Friend
☐ Doctor
☐ Therapist/Coach/Support Group

Do you sometimes smile in a conversation in hopes that it will be a sufficient contribution because you have totally lost track of what is being talked about?

Brandy: Yes. Glad to know I'm not alone.

Godwin: No, I've gotten rather good at masking or talking more than I listen.

Belinda: Yes, a smile and a nod are go-to moves.

Austin: Hahaha. I hope not.

Toshi: Yes, I have. And I'm actually good at doing that.

Muniqui: No.

Sara: Yes and no. I jump in with, "Hold on. I missed that last point!"

Nathan: Yes. I do my best impression of a person who enjoys small talk.

Q 116

Do you find it difficult to explain the rules of a game, not because you don't know them but because you just can't stand the laborious process of reviewing them, step-by-step?

☐ YES
☐ NO

If yes, how does your impatience when explaining complex rules . . .			
• Affect how you feel about yourself?	☐	☐	☐
• Play a role in your relationship(s)?	☐	☐	☐
• Show up in your work/school?	☐	☐	☐
• Impact your ability to make future plans?	☐	☐	☐

What are some examples of when this has happened?

When is this a positive trait, and when is this a negative one?

Note to share this page with . . . .

☐ Family/Partner
☐ Friend
☐ Doctor
☐ Therapist/Coach/Support Group

Do you find it difficult to explain the rules of a game, not because you don't know them but because you just can't stand the laborious process of reviewing them, step-by-step?

Brandy: Yes. Sometimes.

Godwin: It depends on the game; if it's the Game of Life, I don't know those rules.

Belinda: No, I don't mind explaining rules of a game so it can be an enjoyable experience for everyone.

Austin: Yes.

Toshi: Yes, I am. I often picture things rather than understand them logically, so explaining the steps is difficult for me sometimes.

Muniqui: No.

Sara: Correct!

Nathan: Definitely.

Q 117

Do you often feel resistant or frustrated when asked to do something that at first doesn't seem logical or necessary to you?

☐ YES
☐ NO

If yes, how does this . . .			
• Affect how you feel about yourself?	☐	☐	☐
• Play a role in your relationship(s)?	☐	☐	☐
• Show up in your work/school?	☐	☐	☐
• Impact your ability to make future plans?	☐	☐	☐

What has helped you push through your frustration and do the thing you are asked?

What are other examples of when you resist doing something you are being asked to do, and why do you resist?

Note to share this page with . . . .

☐ Family/Partner
☐ Friend
☐ Doctor
☐ Therapist/Coach/Support Group

Do you often feel resistant or frustrated when asked to do something that at first doesn't seem logical or necessary to you?

Brandy: I am immediately frustrated when asked to do something I perceive as illogical or unnecessary. I often find it super hard not to state that fact and why I feel as I do.

Godwin: Yes, very much! My first (automatic) "thought" to requests is usually a "No!" But then that can switch to problem-solving and or my recommendations. Although I don't know if that's for a quick resolution for me or a better outcome for the requestee. I think it's the former. Unfortunately, I usually say "Yes" to most requests, despite myself.

Belinda: Yes, I feel encumbered when asked to do something that seems illogical or unnecessary. I usually ask questions about the purpose and offer suggestions for improvements.

Austin: I would agree with that. I definitely like to understand a process fully and do things my way and then maybe overtime I might discover that the thing I was resisting was actually right, but I had to go through a full self-discovery phase to learn on my own to come to the same conclusion later.

Toshi: Yes, very often. If something doesn't make sense to me or feel logical, I tend to experience an emotional resistance first. However, once I understand and agree with the reasoning, my focus can actually become extremely strong.

Muniqui: Absolutely, completely, 100 percent, and this is one of the biggest frustrations that I have, that when I ask the questions, people do not answer in a way that makes sense. They think they're speaking logically, and I'm telling them what you're telling me doesn't make sense and I don't follow, and they look at me like I have an arm growing out of my head.

Sara: Yes, I definitely do. I want to make everyone understand why it's illogical.

Nathan: *Resistant* or *frustrated* would describe how I feel in these situations on my best days. I have an embarrassingly low tolerance for anything I don't see as being purposeful. I aim to spend as much of my time doing what only I can do, and I actively avoid anything that doesn't align with that intention.

Q 118

No matter how hard you try to be on time, do you usually arrive late?

☐ YES
☐ NO

If yes, how does arriving late . . .

• Affect how you feel about yourself?	☐	☐	☐
• Play a role in your relationship(s)?	☐	☐	☐
• Show up in your work/school?	☐	☐	☐
• Impact your ability to make future plans?	☐	☐	☐

What are some examples of when this has happened?

When is this a positive trait, and when is this a negative one?

Note to share this page with . . . .

☐ Family/Partner
☐ Friend
☐ Doctor
☐ Therapist/Coach/Support Group

No matter how hard you try to be on time, do you usually arrive late?

Brandy: Yes.

Godwin: Yes. Usually by five minutes exactly. Or I'm thirty minutes early.

Belinda: Yes! I call it "Latin time" and almost always arrive fashionably late, despite my efforts to be on time.

Austin: Not early on, but eventually, yes.

Toshi: No, I don't think so. I manage my time fairly normally.

Muniqui: *Yes!*

Sara: Yep. I have shame about this.

Nathan: Often, yes.

Q 119

Do you hope that your children never have to go through what you went through as a child with ADHD and what you go through now?

☐ YES
☐ NO

If yes, how do your childhood experiences . . .

• Affect how you feel about yourself?	☐	☐	☐
• Play a role in your relationship(s)?	☐	☐	☐
• Show up in your work/school?	☐	☐	☐
• Impact your ability to make future plans?	☐	☐	☐

What are some examples of when this has happened?

When is this a positive trait, and when is this a negative one?

Note to share this page with . . . .

☐ Family/Partner
☐ Friend
☐ Doctor
☐ Therapist/Coach/Support Group

Do you hope that your children never have to go through what you went through as a child with ADHD and what you go through now?

Brandy: Yes.

Godwin: Yes, but I have an older daughter, and she definitely isn't suffering; she makes me suffer.

Belinda: My teenager is autistic and has ADHD. Seeing many similarities in his childhood prompted me to get diagnosed.

Austin: No.

Toshi: No. I actually hope they experience hard things while they are young, because I believe those experiences will make them tougher.

Muniqui: Yes.

Sara: This one hits me. I know they will. Five years ago, I would have proudly said that I have the tools to avoid this for them. I was wrong. I can't teach them everything. Plus, I am flawed. But I will be able to minimize it.

Nathan: Absolutely. When I notice certain behaviors in my children, I try to share some of the strategies, systems, and tactics that have helped me. Occasionally, they listen.

Q 120

Do you tend to be very transparent or honest in conversations, in which other people remark on your candor?

☐ YES
☐ NO

If yes, how does your need to move on to the next activity . . .

			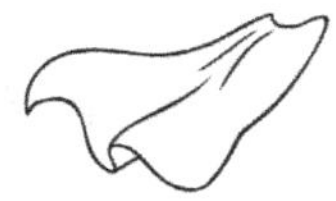
• Affect how you feel about yourself?	☐	☐	☐
• Play a role in your relationship(s)?	☐	☐	☐
• Show up in your work/school?	☐	☐	☐
• Impact your ability to make future plans?	☐	☐	☐

What are some examples of when this has happened?

When is this a positive trait, and when is this a negative one?

Note to share this page with . . . .

☐ Family/Partner
☐ Friend
☐ Doctor
☐ Therapist/Coach/Support Group

Do you tend to be very transparent or honest in conversations, in which other people remark on your candor?

Brandy: Yes. Depending on the audience. I can be very transparent. I don't like people I think are being deceptive, so I try to be as honest and forthcoming as possible.

Godwin: Maybe more when I was younger. I was a bit of a blurter and often the recipient of a furrowed brow or an awkward silence. As I've gotten older, I find it's better not to offer unsolicited opinions or judgments. Pros: Seeing no facial gymnastics. Cons: I will ramble on about whatever I want to ramble on about.

Belinda: Yes, I'm quite transparent in conversations and tend to overshare, especially if I can relate to a topic. My son has mentioned it a couple of times. Ouch!

Austin: I'm very honest with friends and family, and at work, I always say what's on my mind and try to be polite and friendly at all times, but sometimes I can be blunt and direct. I prefer to be honest and transparent versus beating around the bush and having people read between the lines. I like to know where I stand with people.

Toshi: Yes, I do. It's not that I intentionally try to be blunt, but my thoughts tend to come out exactly as they are. It feels more natural for me to express facts or my honest feelings directly rather than using indirect or softened language.

Muniqui: I do that on occasion. I have since learned to try to control that, but it still happens from time to time.

Sara: Wow, yes, this is so true for me.

Nathan: Yes.

Q 121

Do you have trouble lingering? For example, if you see something beautiful, like a sunset or a painting, do you have trouble savoring it for more than a few seconds before you feel the need to move on, even though you liked the sunset or the painting?

☐ YES
☐ NO

If yes, how does impatience to get to the next thing . . .

• Affect how you feel about yourself?	☐	☐	☐
• Play a role in your relationship(s)?	☐	☐	☐
• Show up in your work/school?	☐	☐	☐
• Impact your ability to make future plans?	☐	☐	☐

What are some examples of when this has happened?

When is this a positive trait, and when is this a negative one?

Note to share this page with . . . .

☐ Family/Partner
☐ Friend
☐ Doctor
☐ Therapist/Coach/Support Group

Do you have trouble lingering? For example, if you see something beautiful, like a sunset or a painting, do you have trouble savoring it for more than a few seconds before you feel the need to move on, even though you liked the sunset or the painting?

Brandy: Yes.

Godwin: This question assumes that I noticed it in the first place.

Belinda: No, I enjoy lingering to observe the beauty of something.

Austin: Yes. It's hard to change tasks and get into the next mode.

Toshi: I don't think so. I love beautiful things.

Muniqui: I don't understand the question.

Sara: No, I like to wallow in it awhile.

Nathan: Any time I hear the term "linger," I have to hum the chorus of The Cranberries song. Now that I've done that, the answer is yes . . . I think. I'm still on that song.

Q 122

Do you sometimes get exceedingly annoyed (even if you don't show it) when someone interrupts you while you're watching a video or working on your computer, even though the interruption was intended to be pleasant?

☐ YES
☐ NO

If yes, how does your annoyance at being interrupted . . .			
• Affect how you feel about yourself?	☐	☐	☐
• Play a role in your relationship(s)?	☐	☐	☐
• Show up in your work/school?	☐	☐	☐
• Impact your ability to make future plans?	☐	☐	☐

What are some examples of when this has happened?

When is this a positive trait, and when is this a negative one?

Note to share this page with . . . .

☐ Family/Partner
☐ Friend
☐ Doctor
☐ Therapist/Coach/Support Group

Do you sometimes get exceedingly annoyed (even if you don't show it) when someone interrupts you while you're watching a video or working on your computer, even though the interruption was intended to be pleasant?

Brandy: Yes.

Godwin: I mean, how can you get annoyed at a pleasant interruption? If it were not a pleasant interruption, I'd probably be annoyed.

Belinda: Yes, I get bothered by any interruptions if I'm immersed in reading or on the computer.

Austin: Yes.

Toshi: Yes, sometimes. When I'm really concentrating, interruptions make me feel annoyed.

Muniqui: *Yes!*

Sara: Not really. Maybe I've been trained by now, because children?

Nathan: I get terribly annoyed when I'm interrupted doing pretty much anything. It's a problem.

If you made it this far into this quiz, are you surprised that you have paid attention this long?

☐ YES
☐ NO

If yes, does your usual habit of not finishing things . . .

• Affect how you feel about yourself?	☐	☐	☐
• Play a role in your relationship(s)?	☐	☐	☐
• Show up in your work/school?	☐	☐	☐
• Impact your ability to make future plans?	☐	☐	☐

What is something else you can focus on for long periods of time?

When is this a positive trait, and when is this a negative one?

Note to share this page with . . . .

☐ Family/Partner
☐ Friend
☐ Doctor
☐ Therapist/Coach/Support Group

If you made it this far into this quiz, are you surprised that you have paid attention this long?

Brandy: Yes. Deadline.

Godwin: No, not really. I'm still in deadline mode, so I have to finish it.

Belinda: No, these questions are quite eye-opening.

Austin: I tend to hyperfocus once I have committed.

Toshi: Yes. I'm surprised that I made it through this so quickly.

Muniqui: No. I spread it out over a few days, so it was manageable.

Sara: No. I get to talk about myself.

Nathan: Not really. This has been fun. These questions make me feel seen and understood.

Do you often open your microwave only to find old food or drinks you forgot to take out?

☐ YES
☐ NO

If yes, how does being forgetful . . .

• Affect how you feel about yourself?	☐	☐	☐
• Play a role in your relationship(s)?	☐	☐	☐
• Show up in your work/school?	☐	☐	☐
• Impact your ability to feed yourself food on a regular schedule?	☐	☐	☐

What are some examples of when this has happened?

When is this a positive trait, and when is this a negative one?

Note to share this page with . . . .

☐ Family/Partner
☐ Friend
☐ Doctor
☐ Therapist/Coach/Support Group

Do you often open your microwave only to find old food or drinks you forgot to take out?

Brandy: Sometimes. This one is not as bad because my microwave beeps until I take the food out!

Godwin: Very rarely. My ping is quite loud! Shout-out to Kenwood. They know how to make a microwave!

Belinda: Yes, that happens with my tea. Also with the oven. I've left side dishes in the oven until the next day a few times.

Austin: That doesn't happen to me very often. I'm pretty food-motivated.

Toshi: Yes, I do. I feel like I don't have an internal "check" function. Instead, that function exists outside of me—usually in other people. When someone points out, "Whose drink is this?" or "Who left this lunch box in the microwave?", that's when I realize it. If nobody says anything, I have no check function at all. Microwaves should have—or be developed with—a better alarm function for people like me.

Muniqui: No, I don't.

Sara: Yep! But now my microwave beeps till I take it out.

Nathan: No. My hunger, thirst, or desire for caffeine generally overrides my forgetfulness.

Even if you don't talk about them much, do you think about the big questions in life more than you imagine the average person does?

☐ YES
☐ NO

If yes, how does your focus on big questions in life . . .

• Affect how you feel about yourself?	☐	☐	☐
• Play a role in your relationship(s)?	☐	☐	☐
• Show up in your work/school?	☐	☐	☐
• Impact your ability to make future plans?	☐	☐	☐

What are some examples of when this has happened?

When is this a positive trait, and when is this a negative one?

Note to share this page with . . . .

☐ Family/Partner
☐ Friend
☐ Doctor
☐ Therapist/Coach/Support Group

Even if you don't talk about them much, do you think about the big questions in life more than you imagine the average person does?

Brandy: Yes.

Godwin: No, I don't think so. I need to think more about the bigger questions or at least try to answer them.

Belinda: Yes, I do believe I think about the big life questions more than others. I was also like that as a child.

Austin: Yes.

Toshi: Yes. And I love discussing those big questions.

Muniqui: Yes.

Sara: I think about them a lot, but I always thought everyone did.

Nathan: Back to this idea of "average" . . . I think considering the big questions in life is characteristic of anyone who aspires to live an intentional, introspective existence. I try to spend as much time as possible with such people and tend to avoid those who seem to just shuffle through life.

Do you feel a great deal of secret shame about how disorganized you are?

☐ YES
☐ NO

If yes, how does your shame . . .			
• Affect how you feel about yourself?	☐	☐	☐
• Play a role in your relationship(s)?	☐	☐	☐
• Show up in your work/school?	☐	☐	☐
• Impact your ability to make future plans?	☐	☐	☐

What are some examples of when this has happened?

When is this a positive trait, and when is this a negative one?

Note to share this page with . . . .

☐ Family/Partner
☐ Friend
☐ Doctor
☐ Therapist/Coach/Support Group

Do you feel a great deal of secret shame about how disorganized you are?

Brandy: Yes.

Godwin: I have a great deal of secret shame about many things.

Belinda: No, I don't feel ashamed because I tend to be quite organized. I believe my upbringing didn't allow for disorganization.

Austin: Just around my career.

Toshi: It's hard to hide in my case. Yes, I do have those feelings. I mess things up so much that even the search engine on my PC can't find the file I need.

Muniqui: Yes.

Sara: So much. See above. Rivers of shame.

Nathan: I have learned that I go to shame in any area of my life that isn't where I think it should be. It's something I'm working on.

Q 127

Even though the questions in this quiz are diverse, can you intuit the theme that ties them all together, even if you can't explain it logically in words?

☐ YES
☐ NO

If yes, how does relating to the questions in this quiz . . .

• Affect how you feel about yourself?	☐	☐	☐
• Play a role in your relationship(s)?	☐	☐	☐
• Show up in your work/school?	☐	☐	☐
• Impact your ability to make future plans?	☐	☐	☐

What are some examples of when this has happened?

When is this a positive trait, and when is this a negative one?

Note to share this page with . . . .

☐ Family/Partner
☐ Friend
☐ Doctor
☐ Therapist/Coach/Support Group

Even though the questions in this quiz are diverse, can you intuit the theme that ties them all together, even if you can't explain it logically in words?

Brandy: Yes.

Godwin: I haven't really thought about it. I'm just answering the questions one by one, assuming they're related to ADHD.

Belinda: Yes, I do see a theme that ties these questions together. It's our little secret.

Austin: Yes. Mostly because I have done lots of personal work around my status.

Toshi: Yes, I can. That theme is basically who I am.

Muniqui: Yes. They are all signs and symptoms of ADHD.

Sara: Yes, but I think I could probably also put it into words. But maybe because it's my craft. I worked for decades honing that skill (journalism).

Nathan: Yes. I think I may actually be able to put it into words as well, but that would take more time and space than I have at this moment. It's also not the question being asked . . . so I'll move on.

Q 128

Was there a point during this quiz when you said to yourself, "Wow—this is me"?

☐ YES
☐ NO

If yes, how does connecting to these themes of ADHD . . .

• Affect how you feel about yourself?	☐	☐	☐
• Play a role in your relationship(s)?	☐	☐	☐
• Show up in your work/school?	☐	☐	☐
• Impact your ability to make future plans?	☐	☐	☐

What are some examples of when this has happened?

When is this a positive trait, and when is this a negative one?

Note to share this page with . . . .

☐ Family/Partner
☐ Friend
☐ Doctor
☐ Therapist/Coach/Support Group

Was there a point during this quiz when you said to yourself, "Wow—this is me"?

Brandy: Yes!

Godwin: Oh, I knew Ned knew. We go way back (a shameless name-drop).

Belinda: Yes, that happened various times, and I smiled to myself.

Austin: These questions my diagnosis for sure.

Toshi: Yes. All 128 Questions felt like they were asking about me.

Muniqui: I expected these questions to be like this since they are from ADHD experts.

Sara: *Yes*, I can't believe it! So much of it. The wanting to hug someone while they're talking is still blowing my mind.

Nathan: Absolutely. Arriving at my ADHD diagnosis has been one of the most helpful realizations of my adult life. It helped me make sense of so many things that had previously confused and frustrated me to no end. Today, I am grateful for the many positive aspects that being the way I am has made possible. I truly believe it to be a superpower that we all have the ability to harness in unique and beautiful ways.

WHAT'S NEXT?

NOW THAT YOU have taken the 128 Questions (or you flipped to the back of the book to see the punch line), what is next? My hope is that your journey through the questions helped you get a sense of your past—so that you can see yourself more clearly.

1. **Reflect on how ADHD may have shaped your experiences.** As you moved through this book, my hope is that your story began to feel more coherent, your experiences are more valid, and your inner voice now feels a little less harsh.

2. **Open space for new, deeper, and more honest conversations with friends and your family/partner—the circle of people in your life**.

This workbook can help you share your experience and be seen as a part of a larger group of people who may struggle with similar issues and have similar strengths. There is something uniquely powerful—and deeply healing—about being in shared space, whether in person or online, with people who see you and truly *get* you. Being understood in this way has a way of softening self-judgment and reminding us that we were never meant to do this alone.

This shared space can begin simply. It might start with a conversation with a friend over a cup of tea or a walk on a beach. Bring the workbook and share any questions that were eye-opening for you. It might take shape in an online post (on our website **128ADHD.com** or use hashtags **#128ADHD**), a group chat, or a book group reading this book.

You may also choose to work through this book with a therapist. Bringing specific questions into the session can offer a clear and gentle way to talk about experiences that are often hard to put into words. For many people, this shared reflection deepens understanding, strengthens self-compassion, and helps connect insight to meaningful change.

3. **And in the end, now that you have this framework, how can it serve as a gateway to find other people with ADHD, building a new group of friends and support?** There is something profoundly powerful and healing about being in shared space—virtual or physical—with other people who think this way.

You might invite a few friends over who you imagine might be "neurospicy" and use questions as an icebreaker or party game—curious to see who recognizes themselves immediately and who finds the questions baffling or oddly disconnected. Both responses can be revealing.

In new groups or in your family, may your reflections help you find that humor often lives alongside understanding. I truly believe that if we can laugh together, we can see our human failings and quiet the criticism that is deep in our core. With time, self-love replaces self-blame. We are the only people we have, and to quote from many social media posts, *No one is coming to save us.*

As we hold the more challenging aspects of ADHD care and compassion, we can open our hearts and recognize and celebrate the creativity, insight, intensity, and unique strengths we share. My hope is that you take these questions beyond the pages of this book and into your everyday life. Use them to spark conversation, recognize shared traits, and find others who experience the world in similar ways. Most of all, I hope you keep connecting—with curiosity, openness, and kindness toward yourself and others.

May you find joy in the humor, creativity, and intensity of our unique yet familiar brains. And may those connections remind you, again and again, that you belong.

May the 128 Questions help you understand where you've been.

May the 128 Questions help you feel seen and acknowledged.

And may the 128 Questions bring understanding that supports you in loving yourself as you move forward.

BEHIND THE QUESTIONS

FOR READERS WHO want to know more.

Are you the kind of person who likes to understand what sits beneath the surface?

If so, this chapter is for you. Some readers finish the 128 Questions feeling seen and satisfied. Others want more context—clinical, scientific, and conceptual. The following pages are designed to offer that deeper layer of understanding while keeping the spirit of reflection that guided this book.

Are the 128 Questions an official test?

No. The 128 Questions are not a diagnostic test. Only a trained clinician can formally diagnose ADHD. These questions were originally written in 2005, as a way of introducing readers to the general terrain of ADHD—its challenges, paradoxes, and lived realities. They have been updated for this book.

Their purpose is not to diagnose but to help you reflect on patterns in your life that may warrant deeper exploration.

Can the 128 Questions help me officially diagnose myself with ADHD?

No. While many readers recognize themselves in these questions, self-recognition alone does not constitute a medical diagnosis. A formal ADHD diagnosis requires a comprehensive evaluation conducted by a qualified professional. This typically includes clinical interviews, developmental history, functional impairment assessment, and sometimes standardized rating scales.

This book is designed to provide insight, language, and reflection—not diagnosis.

Where can I find the official elements needed for the diagnosis of ADHD?

The official diagnostic criteria for ADHD are outlined in the *Diagnostic and Statistical Manual of Mental Disorders, Fifth Edition, Text Revision (DSM-5-TR)*, published by the American Psychiatric Association, 2022. The DSM is the primary clinical reference used by mental health professionals in the United States and many other countries. It is periodically updated as research and clinical understanding evolve.

What are the official DSM criteria for ADHD?

According to the DSM-5-TR, ADHD is classified as a neurodevelopmental disorder defined by persistent patterns of inattention and/or hyperactivity-impulsivity that interfere with functioning or development (American Psychiatric Association, 2022).

Symptoms must

- Begin before age twelve
- Persist for at least six months
- Occur in two or more settings (e.g., home, school, work)
- Cause functional impairment

The DSM organizes ADHD symptoms into two primary categories.
Category 1: Inattention

These symptoms include

- Carelessness about details or frequent mistakes
- Difficulty sustaining attention
- Appearing not to listen when spoken to directly
- Failing to follow through on instructions
- Problems with organization
- Avoiding tasks requiring sustained mental effort
- Losing necessary items
- Being easily distracted
- Forgetfulness in daily activities

These patterns often affect academic, occupational, and daily functioning.
Category 2: Hyperactivity & Impulsivity

These symptoms include

- Fidgeting or restlessness
- Leaving one's seat when expected to remain seated
- Running or climbing inappropriately *(in adults, this may present as inner restlessness)*
- Difficulty engaging quietly in activities
- Feeling constantly "on the go"
- Talking excessively
- Blurting out answers
- Difficulty waiting one's turn
- Interrupting or intruding on others

In adults, these symptoms often appear more subtly but can still significantly affect daily life.

Diagnostic criteria summarized from the *Diagnostic and Statistical Manual of Mental Disorders* (5th ed., text rev.; DSM-5-TR) (American Psychiatric Association, 2022).

How does the DSM definition of ADHD compare to the 128 Questions?

The DSM focuses on impairment—identifying symptoms that interfere with functioning. The 128 Questions explore something broader: How ADHD is lived. While the DSM organizes ADHD into two diagnostic clusters—inattention and hyperactivity/impulsivity—lived experience extends far beyond these categories. The questions in this book explore attention, restlessness, impulsivity, emotional intensity, creativity, relationships, identity, and life impact—not through clinical evaluation but through personal reflection.

Everything else in ADHD literature (creativity, emotionality, novelty-seeking, etc.) lives outside formal diagnostic coding—but is still clinically recognized.

Both perspectives matter. One defines ADHD medically. The other helps you understand what it has meant in your life. In this way, the 128 Questions examine not just whether ADHD exists but what it feels like to live with it.

What do the 128 Questions explore that is not in the DSM?

Where the DSM asks, "Is there impairment?"

The 128 Questions ask**, "How has ADHD shaped a life?"**

This includes areas not fully captured in formal diagnostic criteria, such as the following:

- Strengths
- Identity formation
- Relationship patterns
- Meaning-making
- Emotional rhythms
- Creative expression

How do you know that the 128 Questions outside of formal diagnostic criteria are ADHD-related?

In the chapter, "A Spectrum of Traits," in the book, *ADHD 2.0*, Hollowell and Ratey write that ADHD is "a complex set of contradictory or paradoxical tendencies: a lack of focus combined with an ability to hyper focus; a lack of direction combine with a highly directed entrepreneurism; a tendency to procrastinate combined with a knack of getting a week's worth of work done in two hours . . . and the list goes on."

They then list their twenty "telltale signs of ADHD that might send you looking for a clinical confirmation:"

20 Telltale Signs compared to ADHD language used in 2026

Hallowell and Ratey's 20 Telltale Signs	ADHD language in 2026
- Unexplained underachievement	- Executive dysfunction, inconsistent performance
- A wandering mind	- Attention regulation, distractibility, inattentive presentation, default mode network
- Trouble organizing and planning	- Executive dysfunction, prioritization, task initiation, task completion, working mem
- A high degree of creativity and imagination	- Divergent thinking, big-picture thinking
- Trouble with time management and a tendency to procrastinate	- Time blindness, time estimation, transition difficulties
- Strong will / stubbornness / refusal of help	- Cognitive inflexibility, demand avoidance (for some individuals),
- Generosity	- Empathy, compassion
- Restlessness or woolgathering	- Internal hyperactivity, physical restlessness, mind wandering, under-stimulation
- Unique and active sense of humor	- Divergent thinking, creativity, cognitive flexibility
- Trouble sharing and playing with others alongside a desire to make friends	- Social communication differences, social skills, emotional regulation
- Exquisite sensitivity to criticism or rejection	- Rejection sensitivity, rejection sensitive dysphoria (RSD), emotional dysregulation
- Impulsiveness and impatience	- Response inhibition, emotional impulsivity
- An itch to change the conditions of life	- Novelty seeking, stimulation seeking, dopamine-driven motivation
- High energy	- Hyperactivity, energy regulation, intensity
- Uncanny accurate intuition	- Pattern recognition, systems thinking, big-picture thinking
- Transparency to the point of being honest to a fault	- Reduced social filtering, impulsive communication, authenticity
- Susceptibility to addictions and compulsive behaviors of all kinds	- Reward dysregulation, dopamine seeking, impulsivity, compulsive behaviors
- Being a metaphorical lightning rod and weather vane	- Emotional dysregulation, emotional intensity, sensory issues, environmental sensitiv
- Tendency to externalize or blame others or not see your role in the problem	- Emotional regulation challenges, self-awareness, self-monitoring, attribution bias, accountability
- Distorted negative self-image	- Cognitive flexibility, low self-esteem, shame, Imposter syndrome, self-criticism

Why is a trait in ADHD often thought of in terms of being a pair—something that can show up as a positive or a negative in a person's life?

In their book, *ADHD 2.0*, Dr. Edward Hallowell and Dr. John Ratey describe this duality in ADHD as a **"condition of paradoxical pairs"** (Hallowell & Ratey, 2021). ADHD traits often exist in dual form—both challenging and advantageous depending on context. And from this chapter in *ADHD 2.0*, "That's why living with ADHD can be such a mishmash, so confusing, but also exciting and sometimes groundbreaking."

For example, the following:

- Distractibility ↔ Curiosity
- Impulsivity ↔ Spontaneity
- Hyperfocus ↔ Difficulty shifting attention
- Emotional intensity ↔ Passion

Living with ADHD can feel confusing because strengths and struggles are intertwined. Yet this same paradox is also a source of creativity, innovation, and resilience.

Here is a chart from *ADHD 2.0* (reprinted with permission from the authors):

USEFUL	PROBLEMATIC
Tenacious; never gives up; will literally collapse before quitting	Stubborn; would rather fail doing it their way than succeed taking advice from someone else; can spend a lifetime trying to get good at what he or she's bad at
Can act on the spur of the moment	Procrastination can be a huge problem
Original; sees solutions others do not; comes up with novel ideas	Can seem whacky, eccentric, even crazy; can put people off by being too offbeat and arrogant
Confident; self-assured	Insecure; feels success was all done by smoke and mirrors
Extremely hardworking	Driven; compulsive; can't let up; maniacal
Lightning-quick mind	Trouble shutting mind down; risk of developing addictions to quiet mind down
Risk taker; focuses and performs best in situations of crisis and danger	Needs danger to feel engaged with life and truly alive
Sees the big picture before anyone else	Trouble with implementation and sweating the details
Generous; bighearted; willing to give with no expectation of return	Can give away the store
Funny; the life of the party; can connect with everyone	Secretly lonely; feels no one really knows them
Innovator	Can't/won't follow instructions
Pays close attention when interested	Easily distracted; mind wanders when not interested; frequently on electronic devices and difficult to engage
Supremely talented in several domains	Seriously limited in other domains
A life enthusiast; wants to try everything; can't ever get enough	Overcommitted; about to snap
Strong leader; charismatic	Hates the position of leader; worries he or she will let everyone down; unaware of his or her own charisma
Thrives in highly stimulating situations	Finds contentment too bland and so can disrupts ordinary happiness in order to create high stimulation
Loves debate, conflict, sparring	Intimacy can be difficult unless partner likes these as well

USEFUL	PROBLEMATIC
Passionate; zealous; idealistic; sacrifices for a cause or a friend	Can become rigid, fanatical, strident, irrational, strident, irrational, Captain Ahab Syndrome
Meticulous at times, especially on projects that matter a great deal	Usually disorganized, even chaotically so: chaos can rule to such an extent that school, job, marriage hang in the balance
Can get a lot done in a short amount of time	Fundamentally different sense of time; there is only NOW and NOT NOW in this world, so procrastination rules; and things rarely get done on time
An appreciation of the offbeat, unusual, unconventional	An inability or refusal to conform or get in line when doing so is obviously in his or her best interest
Dreamer par excellence; visionary; lives on wings of imagination: flights of fancy	Sometimes so bored by reality that he or she ginores it and gets into trouble for having done so
Honest to a fault; will say what others don't dare to say; outspoken; blunt	Can hurt feelings and damage self, can unwittingly be cruel, which is the last thing he or she wants to be
Intense desire to be free and independent, own boss; master of own fate	Trouble working on teams; trouble taking orders: trouble with intimact in private life
Naturally creative; ideas pop all the time like in a pop corn machine	Trouble organizing ideas and doing something productive with them
Naturally curious; always wanting to know who, what, where, why, and how: never satisfied until he or she gets the answer	Easily distracted by novelty or any puzzles, conundrum, unsolved problem, or beguiling opportunity, however irrelevant it may be
Enormously energetic; seemingly indefatigable	Impulsive; can't sit still or linger over a conversation or ponder an idea with a colleague or a relative
Mind like a steel trap; can remember details from years ago	Forgets what he and she went into the next room to get; forgets where he and she put car keys;forgets waqllet, glasses, umbrella, leaves groceries on roof of car and drives off
Full of ideas	Too many ideas they choke the growth of any single one
Decisive; can make an important, complex decision in a split second	Impatient; hates to wrestle with ambiguity; shoots from the hip
Initial surge of excitement over new plan, deal, idea, project, relationship	Excitement peters out in the middle phase; trouble sustaining interest
Takes responsibility; gets done what needs to get done	Trouble delegating; trusting that others to do it as well as he or she can

Hallowell, E. M., & Ratey, J. J. (2021). *ADHD 2.0: New Science and Essential Strategies for Thriving with Distraction—from Childhood Through Adulthood.*

How do the 128 Questions compare to Hollowell and Ratey's twenty telltale signs of ADHD?

When the 128 Questions were mapped to the twenty telltale signs of ADHD, every question mapped onto one or more of these signs.

	128 Questions reflecting a "telltale sign"	
	# of questions	% of total questions
Trouble organizing and planning	19	15%
A wandering mind	14	11%
A high degree of creativity and imagination	14	11%
Trouble with time management and a tendency to procrastinate	12	9%
High energy	11	9%
Impulsiveness and impatience	9	7%
Distorted negative self-image	8	6%
Strong will / stubbornness / refusal to help	7	6%
Uncanny accurate intuition	6	5%
Unique and active sense of humor	5	4%
Generosity	3	2%
An itch to change the conditions of life	3	2%
Being a metaphorical lightning rod and weather vane	3	2%
Exquisite sensitivity to criticism or rejection	3	2%
Unexplained underachievement	2	2%
Restlessness or "woolgathering"	2	2%
Early trouble sharing and playing with others alongside a desire to make frie	2	2%
Susceptibility to addictions and compulsive behaviors of all kinds	2	2%
Transparency to the point of being honest to a fault	2	2%
	127 *	100%

* note = one question is blank on 128 questions so there are actually 127

Hallowell, E. M., & Ratey, J. J. (2021). *ADHD 2.0: New science and essential strategies for thriving with distraction*

Many of the traits explored in this book may be impairing in some contexts and advantageous in others. These questions and the personal comments demonstrate how the "disordered aspects of ADHD" can in some certain situations be gifts or superpowers. This duality or set of pairs (positive and negative aspects of a trait) is central to understanding ADHD.

Why aren't the 128 Questions grouped into sections like "memory" or "attention?"

I'm including this question because it was the one that I was asked the most by editors and publishers who looked at this book. And I think in some ways this question really highlights the difference between people who are ADHD and people who are not.

The answer lies in the design of the original questions. One of the brilliant features of Dr. Hallowell's original structure is that the questions are intentionally interwoven rather than thematically grouped. I made sure the updated questions also were interwoven and not thematically grouped.

- This creates several effects:
- The reader never knows what question is coming next.
- Curiosity remains activated.
- Pattern recognition happens organically.
- Engagement is sustained across all 128 items.

In many ways, the structure mirrors the ADHD mind itself—nonlinear, associative, and full of unexpected connections. The experience of moving through the questions becomes part of the insight. Not knowing what comes next keeps the reader turning pages—and often recognizing themselves along the way.

What can the 128 Questions offer a reader beyond the DSM diagnosis?

If the DSM diagnosis provides the diagnostic map, the 128 Questions provide the lived journey. Both are valuable. One names the condition. The other helps you understand what it has meant—and continues to mean—in your own life.

Wherever this exploration leads you next—to diagnosis, deeper understanding, or simply greater self-compassion—it is *your* own exploration that matters.

BOOKS BY DR. NED HALLOWELL

Dr. Ned Hallowell's work has been foundational in shaping modern understanding of ADHD through a strengths-based, lifespan, and lived-experience lens. The books below offer a deeper exploration of diagnosis, relationships, productivity, and thriving with ADHD.

Core ADHD Titles

***Driven to Distraction* (1994)**
with John J. Ratey—A groundbreaking introduction to ADHD in children and adults that helped bring widespread recognition to the condition.

***Delivered from Distraction* (2005)**
with John J. Ratey—An updated, practical guide to living successfully with ADHD across the lifespan.

***ADHD 2.0* (2021)**
with John J. Ratey—A modern synthesis of neuroscience and clinical insight, introducing concepts such as "paradoxical pairs" and interest-based nervous system regulation.

ADHD in Work & Daily Functioning

***Driven to Distraction at Work* (2015)**
with John J. Ratey—Focuses on productivity, organization, and career success for adults with ADHD.

Parenting & Development

***Superparenting for ADD* (2008)**
with Peter S. Jensen—A strengths-oriented parenting guide for raising children with ADHD.

***The Childhood Roots of Adult Happiness* (2002)**
with Peter S. Jensen—Explores how childhood emotional development shapes adult well-being.

Relationships & Family Life

***Married to Distraction* (2010)**
with Sue George Hallowell & Melissa Orlov—Examines how ADHD affects romantic relationships and offers strategies for connection and repair.

Broader Mental Health & Well-Being

***CrazyBusy* (2006)**
Addresses overwhelm, overcommitment, and attention fragmentation in modern life.

***Connect* (1999)**
Explores the role of human connection in emotional health and resilience.

***Shine* (2011)**
Applies brain science and positive psychology to leadership and performance.

ACADEMIC & CLINICAL REFERENCES

American Psychiatric Association. (2022). *Diagnostic and statistical manual of mental disorders* (5th ed., text rev.; DSM-5-TR). American Psychiatric Publishing.

Hallowell, E. M., & Ratey, J. J. (2021). *ADHD 2.0: New science and essential strategies for thriving with distraction—from childhood through adulthood*. Ballantine Books.

Hallowell, E. M., & Ratey, J. J. (1994). *Driven to distraction: Recognizing and coping with attention deficit disorder*. Pantheon Books.

Hallowell, E. M., & Ratey, J. J. (2005). *Delivered from distraction: Getting the most out of life with attention deficit disorder*. Ballantine Books.

CHART REFERENCES

Historical terminology adapted from the diagnostic and historical literature on attention-deficit/hyperactivity disorder. Sources include Crichton's early description of attentional difficulties; Still's lectures on impulsive behavior in children; subsequent psychiatric terminology describing hyperkinetic behavior; and evolving diagnostic terminology in the *Diagnostic and Statistical Manual of Mental Disorders*.

American Psychiatric Association. (1968). *Diagnostic and statistical manual of mental disorders* (2nd ed.). Washington, DC.

American Psychiatric Association. (1980). *Diagnostic and statistical manual of mental disorders* (3rd ed.). Washington, DC.

American Psychiatric Association. (1987). *Diagnostic and statistical manual of mental disorders* (3rd ed., rev.). Washington, DC.

American Psychiatric Association. (2013). *Diagnostic and statistical manual of mental disorders* (5th ed.). Washington, DC.

Barkley, R. A., & Peters, H. (2012). The earliest reference to ADHD in the medical literature? Melchior Adam Weikard's description in 1775 of "attention deficit" (Mangel der aufmerksamkeit, attentio volubilis). Journal of Attention Disorders, 16(8), 623–630. https://doi.org/10.1177/1087054711432309

Crichton, A. (1798/2008). *An inquiry into the nature and origin of mental derangement*. In G. D. Lange, K. W. Lange, S. Reichl, L. Tucha, & O. Tucha (Eds.), historical discussion of attentional disorders.

Lange, K. W., Reichl, S., Lange, K. M., Tucha, L., & Tucha, O. (2010). The history of attention deficit hyperactivity disorder. *Attention Deficit and Hyperactivity Disorders*, 2, 241–255.

Still, G. F. (1902). Some abnormal psychical conditions in children. *The Lancet*, 159(4102), 1008–1012, 1077–1082, 1163–1168.

www.ingramcontent.com/pod-product-compliance
Lightning Source LLC
LaVergne TN
LVHW060027210926
848481LV00013B/3809
* 9 7 9 8 8 9 7 4 7 1 0 4 1 *